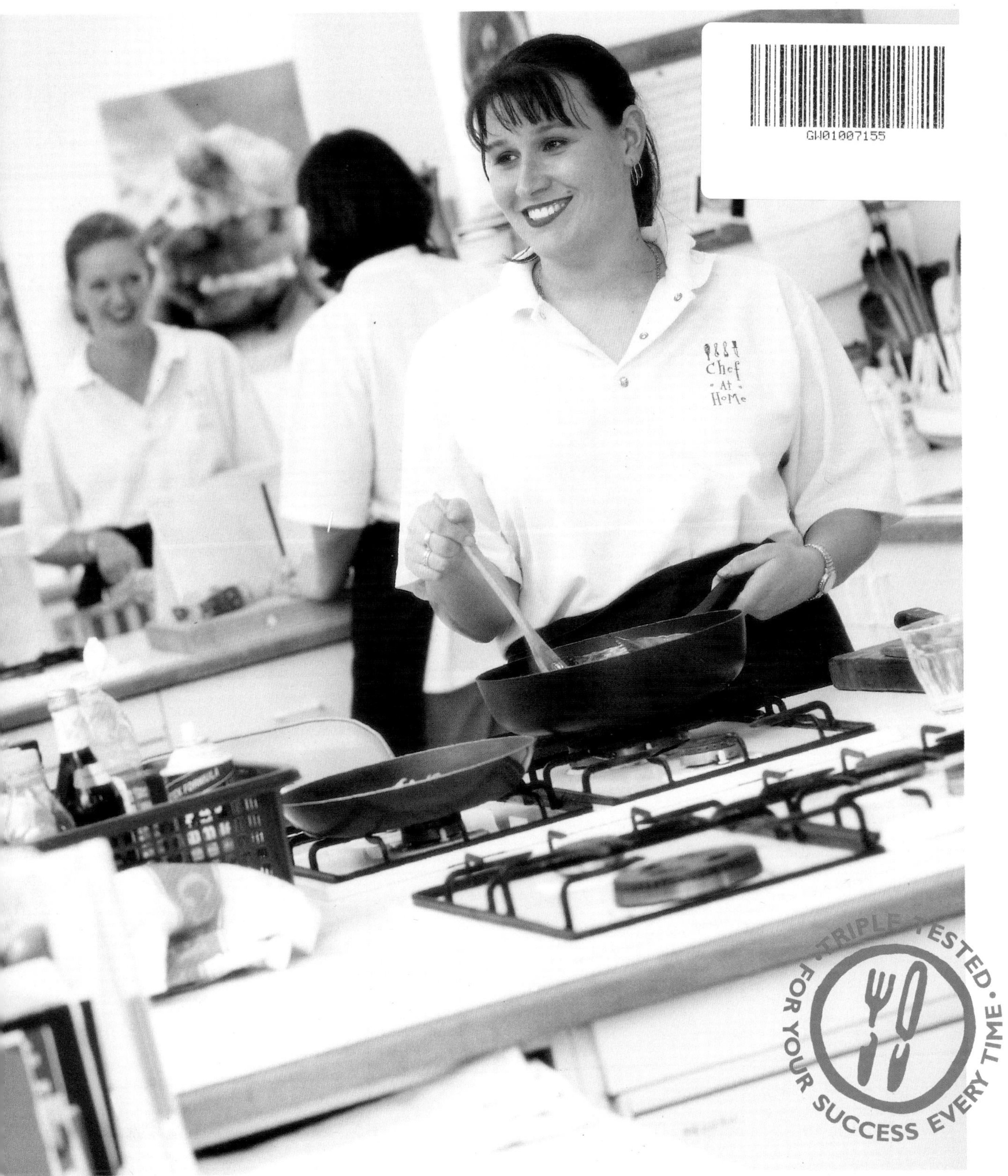

For more than 50 years, *The Australian Women's Weekly* Test Kitchen has been creating marvellous recipes that come with a guarantee of success. First, the recipes always work – just follow the instructions and you too will get the results you see in the photographs. Second, and perhaps more importantly, they are delicious – created by experienced home economists and chefs, all triple-tested and, thanks to their straightforward instructions, easy to make.

POWER LEVELS

All our recipes have been triple-tested in a Panasonic (model number NN-6405) 900-watt microwave oven. Higher wattage ovens cook faster than lower wattage ovens so, since our recipes were made in a 900-watt oven, you'll have to check the instruction booklet of your own microwave oven and adjust cooking times accordingly.

British and North American readers:
Please note that Australian cup and spoon measurements are metric. A quick conversion guide appears on page 119.

The days when busy cooks used their microwave ovens just to reheat leftovers or warm the morning's coffee are long gone. Today's cooks value this essential piece of kitchen equipment for its speed, its ease of use and its versatility. In many cases food can be cooked and served in the same dish – less washing-up is a boon appreciated by all the family – and the range of food which can be produced is practically unlimited.

From soups to main meals, cookies to jams, here are a myriad recipes to make the most of your microwave oven, plus some handy serving suggestions. Starting overleaf, there are hints for using your microwave oven too, with gems of information to make you exclaim, "I'd never have thought of that!" The clever cooks in *The Australian Women's Weekly* Test Kitchen did – and on the following pages they share their secrets and their expertise with you.

Pamela Clark

FOOD EDITOR

contents

the magic of microwaves

We take the mystery out of microwave cooking in this section with preparation and cooking techniques, hints on how to convert conventional recipes for use in the microwave oven, cookware options, tips and much more. Once you master the art of microwave cooking, you'll fall in love with this no-fuss, no-mess style of cooking.

A microwave oven is an essential appliance in every kitchen. You can cook practically anything in a microwave oven today, thanks to the technological advances in their manufacture over the past few years. So, if you're one of the old school who believes that microwave ovens are only good for defrosting or reheating, think again!

Two common complaints about microwave cooking are the lack of browning of meat and the pale, unsavoury appearance of cakes. But there are some simple solutions to these problems.

Meat, even when fully cooked, has a dull, grey appearance. Experienced cooks know how to fix this problem easily with browning agents. No, these browning agents are not special products you'll have to buy. You have a variety of browning products in your pantry, among them soy, teriyaki and barbecue sauces, jams, chutneys and brown sugar. You simply brush the surface of the meat with sauce or a marinade mixture before cooking. Of course, using a recipe that will suit microwave cooking is your best starting point.

A microwave cake *(above)* can look magnificent *(top right)*.

PERFECTING CAKE-BAKING IN YOUR MICROWAVE

Baking cakes in the microwave oven has often led to disappointing results as the cakes tend to be pale in colour and not very appealing.

This is because the porous, airy texture of cakes means they cook in a very short time – and don't brown. But the benefits of baking in the microwave oven – including dramatically reduced baking times, easier recipes and power savings – outweigh the problems. Just choose a recipe that will produce a moist cake and then simply improve the appearance by dusting the cake with icing sugar, cocoa powder or cinnamon sugar. You can also use toasted, shredded or desiccated coconut (before or after cooking), finely chopped toasted nuts (before cooking), or spread the cake with cream cheese frosting, melted chocolate, or icing (after cooking).

preparation and cooking techniques

So what determines how long and how well each food cooks? There are a number of factors involved, among them the size and shape of food, the type of dish used and even how the food is arranged in the dish. Also, one factor many people overlook is that food placed in the microwave oven straight from the refrigerator will take longer to heat than food at room temperature, just as it does with conventional cooking.

Microwave energy

When you turn your microwave oven on, microwaves penetrate the food inside from all angles, causing water and fat molecules in the food to vibrate rapidly. This friction creates the heat that cooks the food. This action continues for some time after the food is removed from the oven, which is why it continues to cook (see Standing Time, page 6). Because food cooks from the outer edges towards the centre, and as microwaves only penetrate to a depth of about 4cm, some recipes may overcook around the outside edges before the centre is done. That's why stirring, turning, shielding and arranging food is so important when cooking in a microwave oven.

Food density and composition

☐ Solid, dense foods (such as meat and potatoes) take longer to cook than airy, porous foods (such as cakes, bread, minced meat).

☐ Fat and sugar attract microwaves, so foods with high levels of either cook and reheat more rapidly, and at a higher temperature, than water-based foods.

☐ Sugary fillings in pies and pastries, cakes and jams become extremely hot much faster than the outside, so take care when testing and eating to avoid being burnt.

☐ Because bones conduct heat, pieces of meat containing bone will cook more quickly than boneless cuts. Also, the section of meat near the bone will cook faster than the rest. That's why you may need to shield the bony part of chops and chicken drumsticks with small pieces of foil to prevent overcooking. See Metal and Aluminium Foil section on page 9 for more details.

Size and shape of food

☐ Smaller pieces of food cook faster than large ones, so it's best to cut your ingredients into similar-size pieces to ensure even cooking. A whole chicken, for example, will cook and begin to dry out around the breast area before the centre is cooked through. Chicken pieces, on the other hand, will cook more evenly.

☐ Food can naturally be an odd shape and may require special attention to ensure even cooking. A fish fillet, for example, may need to be shielded with small pieces of foil at the thinner end to prevent overcooking.

☐ Place the thickest part of fish/meat etc, to the outside of the turntable, where the energy source is greatest, and the thinner end to the middle, or tuck it under.

☐ Do not overload your microwave oven by cooking large amounts of food because the cooking time will increase and the food may not cook evenly.

☐ Cakes should always be cooked in a ring, loaf or shallow, round microwave-safe dish. Make your own microwave-safe ring dish by placing a glass, right-way up, in the centre of a 20cm round microwave-safe dish before you fill it with the cake mixture.

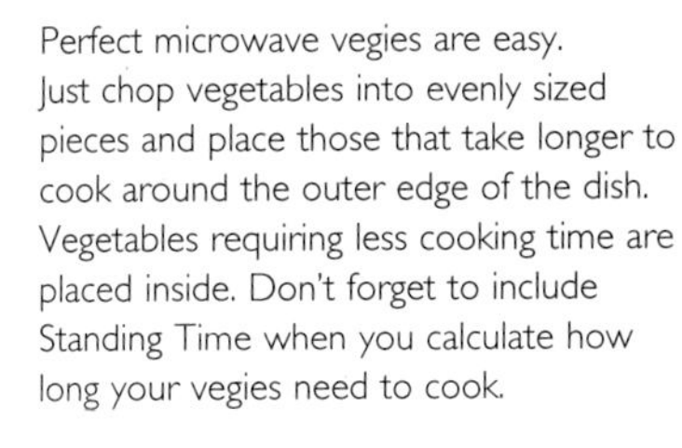

Perfect microwave vegies are easy. Just chop vegetables into evenly sized pieces and place those that take longer to cook around the outer edge of the dish. Vegetables requiring less cooking time are placed inside. Don't forget to include Standing Time when you calculate how long your vegies need to cook.

Arranging and stirring food

Arranging food is just as important as choosing an appropriate dish.

- Arrange food in the microwave oven according to size and shape, with the thickest parts positioned towards the outside of the turntable and thin portions with bone closest to the centre.
- When reheating, make sure that thick, dense pieces of food are towards the outside of the plate or dish.
- Elevating thick cuts of meat on a roasting rack will help even out microwave distribution.
- Stirring foods during cooking is necessary for even heating. Stir from the outside edge of the dish to transfer the food from the centre to the outside.
- Turn thick portions of meat, chicken, vegetables etc, once to ensure they cook evenly.
- Check cakes twice as they bake, as they can cook unevenly. Rotate the pan once during cooking to ensure the whole cake cooks evenly.
- Food with a skin, membrane or other casing should be pierced in several places with a skewer to allow the steam to escape. If the skin is not pierced, the food may burst. Do this to egg yolks when poaching eggs and when cooking sausages, chicken or vegetables with the skin left on.

Standing Time

It's important to remember that food continues to cook after it is removed from the microwave oven because the molecules are still vibrating. That's why many recipes include Standing Times in addition to Cooking Times. Standing Times vary (average is from 5 to 10 minutes) depending on the food. Always test whether your meal is done at the end of the estimated Cooking *and* Standing Time. Then, if extra cooking is necessary, it should be done in short bursts (seconds rather than minutes) to avoid overcooking.

- Cakes will hold heat and continue to cook for a long period because of their high sugar content and airy texture – allow about 10 minutes.
- Meat is treated similarly to when cooked in a conventional oven; it should be slightly undercooked to your preference, then covered and left to stand for 10 to 15 minutes to finish cooking.
- Green vegetables cook quickly and can easily be overcooked in only a few minutes. They should always be cooked covered, unless the recipe states otherwise, and undercooked if they are to be reheated just before serving. Vegetables will remain hot for around 5 minutes if kept covered when removed from the microwave oven.

The use of aluminium foil – around the bone ends of chicken drumsticks and in the corners of a meatloaf – will prevent the food from burning, drying out and overcooking.

Defrosting

Defrosting in the microwave is the quickest and most hygienic way to thaw food. Bacteria does not find the temperature warm and stable enough to grow. The defrost function button is automatically programmed to a medium temperature suitable for defrosting. Foods having high fat content or less density towards the edges, such as minced steak or chicken pieces, attract microwaves and may start to cook around the outside.

The best way to prevent this is to:

1. Place evenly sized, trimmed portions of meat (unwrapped) around the edge of the microwave turntable.
2. Remove any defrosted portions of mince during the defrosting program.

MICROWAVE SAFETY

Microwave oven manufacturers have to adhere to stringent safety standards. Your microwave oven will not operate with the door open and microwaves disappear immediately when the power is turned off. The oven door is fitted with a metal mesh, which reflects the microwaves and prevents any leakage. While the mesh holes are large enough for you to see what's cooking inside, they are too small to allow any waves through. Always follow the manufacturer's instructions for cooking and reheating food in your microwave oven.

Remember, Standing Time must be considered when defrosting. If you leave meat in the microwave oven until it is completely defrosted, it may be half-cooked around the edges. Instead, remove the meat before it thaws out totally and allow about another 15 minutes Standing Time. If larger pieces of meat start to cook around the edges, try using an even lower temperature than defrost, such as LOW (10%), and turn the meat over once during defrosting.

Reheating

Reheating a meal in the microwave oven isn't only convenient – it also saves on washing up, as meals can be ready in minutes on the serving plate. Food taken straight from the refrigerator and placed in the microwave oven will take longer to reheat than food at room temperature. Try using a lower heat setting; it may take a little longer, but the results will reflect the more even heat distribution.

To defrost steaks, place unwrapped, evenly sized, trimmed portions of meat around the edge of the turntable (*top*). When defrosting minced meat (*above*), any defrosted meat should be removed from the microwave oven at intervals throughout the program.

HINTS TO CONVERT CONVENTIONAL RECIPES

You can't convert all recipes to make them suitable for cooking in the microwave oven. Some will look more appealing with a little help from your conventional oven or a quick flash under the grill. But there are many recipes where it's a simple matter of reducing the liquid or cooking time and they'll turn out perfectly. The benefits of your microwave oven in terms of speed, versatility, energy savings and even using fewer dishes is a temptation too good to resist. So, use these hints to adapt or improve conventional recipes and try your favourites in your microwave oven. The results may surprise you.

1 Choose foods with a high moisture content such as fruit, vegetables, mince, chicken, eggs and cheese, as they adapt well to microwave cooking.

2 Reduce the amounts of additional liquid, as far less evaporation occurs in the microwave oven due to the shorter cooking times and the moist environment inside the oven.

3 Browning large cuts of meat is best done on the cooktop then the cooking finished in the microwave oven.

4 Dishes topped with cheese or breadcrumbs should be browned under a grill before serving.

5 As a guide, reduce fats or oils in recipes to a maximum of 40g or 2 tablespoons. Fat and oil are generally used in conventional recipes to prevent food sticking; this doesn't occur in microwave cooking because there is no direct heat.

6 Reduce the addition of flavourings, salt and pepper. Herbs and spices retain more of their flavour due to the shorter cooking times, so use sparingly and add fresh herbs at the end of cooking.

7 As a general rule, reduce cooking times from a conventional recipe for microwave use by about one-third – not forgetting Standing Time. For example, 30 minutes in a conventional oven will be about 20 minutes in the microwave oven. Extra cooking time can be added if necessary but should be done in very short bursts.

8 Recipes which contain cream, eggs, cheese or yogurt should be cooked at a lower temperature than stated in a conventional recipe to prevent curdling. Generally, cook on MEDIUM (55%) or lower when cooking these foods in the microwave oven.

9 It is best to use cake and biscuit recipes designed specifically for microwave cooking, as they are guaranteed. Cook in plastic microwave-safe dishes; plastic does not retain heat and thus prevents overcooking when standing. Cakes cook from the outside in, so ring, loaf and shallow, round microwave-safe dishes must be used to ensure even cooking throughout.

10 Cut food into evenly sized pieces and cook in batches, using smaller dishes, because the microwave oven will not cook evenly if you cook large amounts at the one time.

DOS AND DON'TS

DON'T overcook food. The best advice is to *undercook* all food, check whether the food is done and, if extra cooking is required, do so in very short bursts only.
DON'T shallow- or deep-fry in the microwave oven as the oil can boil and splatter, causing burns.
DO a quick test of all cookware to determine if suitable for use in the microwave oven.
DON'T boil eggs in their shell as they will explode.
DO take care when cooking a whole chicken. After cooking, check the internal temperature has reached 87°C.
DON'T use conventional meat thermometers *inside* a microwave oven. Use them only to test meat temperature after it has been removed from the oven. You can buy microwave thermometers that remain in food during cooking.
DO make sure when shielding food with small amounts of foil that only a maximum of one-third of food is ever covered with the foil.
DON'T ever allow shielding foil or foil trays to touch oven walls, and never cover food entirely with foil.
DO check the wattage of your own microwave oven. Our recipes have been triple-tested in a Panasonic NN-6405 900-watt microwave oven. High-wattage ovens cook faster than low-wattage ovens so, with this in mind, you should adjust cooking times accordingly.

Panasonic NN-6405
900-watt microwave oven.

what cookware to use

You can purchase cookware designed specifically for microwave oven use but you will have suitable cookware in your cupboard. For example, Corningware, Pyrex, glass and some ceramic and plastic dishes are suitable. However, it is important to test any cookware not labelled "microwave-safe".

To test a piece of cookware quickly to determine whether it is safe to use in the microwave oven, fill a microwave-safe jug with 1 cup of cold water. Place it on or alongside the dish to be tested, inside your microwave oven. Heat on HIGH (100%) for 1 minute. If the dish remains cold (while the water is warm), it is safe to use in the microwave oven. If the water is still cool and the dish hot, the dish is not suitable for microwave use. Unsuitable dishes may overheat after a short period of time in the microwave oven and break, warp or cause burns if you remove them without an oven-mitt. Some cookware – including polystyrene and styrofoam containers, bone china, ice-cream and takeaway containers – should only be used for very short periods (2 minutes maximum).

It's best to use round or oval dishes for microwave cooking as the food cooks more evenly. Rectangular or square dishes often need to be shielded with small pieces of foil in the corners to prevent overcooking.

Ovenproof glass

☐ Ordinary glassware, bottles and jars can be used to reheat food for short periods (5 minutes maximum). They are not suitable for general cooking which takes a longer time.

☐ The most useful ovenproof – and microwave-safe – glass is Pyrex, available from large supermarkets, department stores and hardware stores.

China, porcelain and ceramics

Most suitable ovenware dishes will be labelled microwave-safe.

☐ Casserole dishes with glass lids are ideal as they double as serving dishes.

☐ Plastic lids on glass and ceramic cookware are for storage only; they should not be used in the microwave oven unless marked microwave-safe.

☐ Delicate china and dinnerware marked ovenproof is usually safe to use but do not use china with a metallic trim, or containers with metal parts. Do not use any repaired china as the glue will melt.

Stoneware and pottery

☐ Pottery dishes which have been glazed completely inside and out, without any metallic glaze or trim, are suitable for microwave use.

☐ Don't use pottery or stoneware which is not completely covered with glaze unless it is marked microwave-safe, as it may absorb moisture, become extremely hot, cause crazing and eventually crack. If unsure, test to see if it is microwave-safe.

Plastic

☐ Plastic microwave-safe cookware is readily available from large supermarkets or department stores. It is ideal for baking and shorter cooking periods as microwaves transmit through plastic easily. However, some plastic containers may burn or scorch if used for foods with high fat content, such as cheese, or high sugar content, such as jam and sweet fillings.

☐ Melamine dinnerware can be used at low temperatures and for short cooking times (maximum 2 minutes) but may melt or break if overheated.

☐ Ice-cream, takeaway, polystyrene or styrofoam containers can become soft, dangerous to handle and may melt with long cooking times. They should only be used to reheat food for very short periods (maximum 2 minutes).

☐ Most plastic wraps are microwave-safe and can be used. There is a special plastic wrap designed specifically for microwave use. While a little more expensive than conventional plastic wrap, it's worth the investment. When removing plastic wrap from a microwaved dish, carefully peel it from the back of the dish to protect your hands and face from the steam.

☐ Oven bags and some freezer bags can be used; check the manufacturer's instructions. Do not use wire twists in the microwave; cut a narrow strip (about 1cm) off the edge of an oven bag and use this as a tie.

Wood and paper

☐ Wooden bowls or boards shouldn't be used in the microwave oven as they may dry out and crack.

☐ Wicker or straw baskets can be used to warm bread rolls for very short periods; long cooking times will cause any varnish on baskets to crack.

☐ Use wooden skewers in place of metal skewers when cooking kebabs in the microwave oven.

☐ Absorbent papers (like paper towels) can be used for short cooking times to avoid splatters.

☐ Baking paper can be used to prevent food from sticking.

To be safe, always check the manufacturer's instructions for microwave suitability; some recycled brands of paperware may contain metal fragments.

Metal and aluminium foil

☐ Metal cookware, baking dishes or utensils cannot be used in the microwave oven under any circumstances.

☐ Aluminium foil is the only metal-based product that can be used, but only in very small amounts. Never completely cover food with foil; it is only safe to cover up to one-third of food and you must ensure it does not touch the interior walls of the oven.

Because microwaves cannot penetrate foil, small, smooth pieces of foil can be used to shield thin parts of food to prevent overcooking around the edges. Chicken drumsticks, the thin tail-end of fish and the corners of square or rectangular dishes are often shielded for this reason.

☐ Foil trays and containers can be used only when the volume of food is at least double the amount of foil (eg. 70% food to 30% foil) and the container is no more than 2cm high. You must keep the container at least 3cm from the oven walls. Do not use the foil lids that come with foil trays and fold down any sharp edges at the top of the foil container.

☐ Arcing is a term used for sparks which occur when an unsuitable metal utensil or too much foil is used, or the foil container has come in contact with the microwave oven walls. If this occurs, stop the oven immediately, remove the metal or reduce the quantity of foil used. Continued arcing will seriously damage your microwave oven.

A wide range of cookware can be used in your microwave oven.

how do I...

Melt gelatine?
Sprinkle 2 teaspoons of gelatine over 1 tablespoon water in small microwave-safe bowl; cook, uncovered, on MEDIUM (55%) about 30 seconds or until dissolved.

Clarify butter?
Place 125g butter in microwave-safe bowl; cook, uncovered, on MEDIUM-LOW (30%) about 3 minutes or until foaming. Skim foam from surface of butter. Stand butter for 2 minutes before spooning clear liquid into a glass bowl; this clear liquid is the clarified butter.

Toast coconut?
To toast 1/2 cup (45g) coconut, place in a microwave-safe glass dish; cook, uncovered, on HIGH (100%) about 5 minutes or until browned lightly, stirring twice during cooking.

Toast almonds?
To toast 100g slivered, flaked or whole almonds, place in a large, shallow microwave-safe glass dish; cook, uncovered, on HIGH (100%) about 3 minutes or until browned lightly, stirring twice during cooking.

Rehydrate sun-dried tomatoes?
Place 1 cup sun-dried tomatoes in a small microwave-safe glass bowl with 2 tablespoons of red wine or water. Cook, covered, on MEDIUM-HIGH (70%) for 3 minutes, stirring once during cooking.

Pop corn?
Place 1/2 cup (130g) of popping corn in an oven bag or paper bag; secure bag loosely with kitchen string. Place bag on turntable; cook, on MEDIUM-HIGH (70%) for about 4 minutes or until popped. Remove bag from microwave oven with tongs; stand for 2 minutes before opening bag. Sprinkle popcorn with salt to serve.

Soften crystallised honey?
Place jar (without lid) in microwave oven; cook, uncovered, on HIGH (100%) about 30 seconds or until honey liquidises.

Cook pappadums?
Place 2 pappadums at a time on turntable; cook, uncovered, on HIGH (100%) about 30 seconds or until puffed.

Cook prawn crackers?
Place 10 prawn crackers around the edge of turntable; cook, uncovered, on HIGH (100%) about 30 seconds or until puffed.

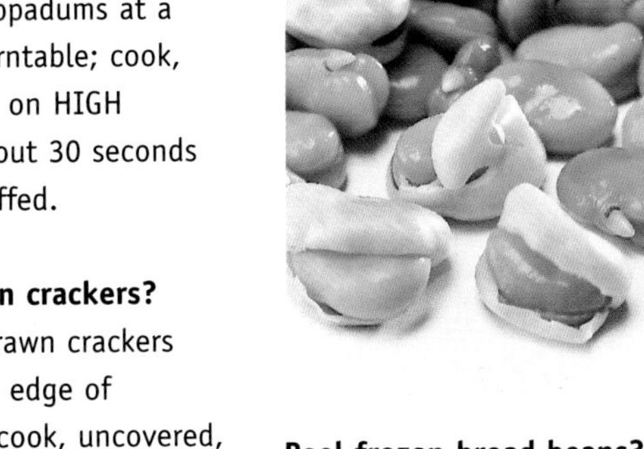

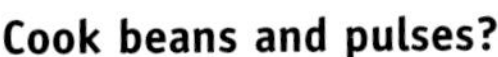

Peel frozen broad beans?
Place 500g frozen broad beans in microwave-safe bowl, cover with cold water; cook, uncovered, on HIGH (100%) about 4 minutes or until tender. Drain, then peel away skin.

Cook beans and pulses?
Rinse and place 1 cup soaked beans or pulses in a large microwave-safe bowl with 4 cups boiling water. Cook, uncovered, on HIGH (100%) for 45 minutes or until tender.

Dry breadcrumbs?
To dry 1 cup (70g) stale breadcrumbs, place on a microwave-safe glass plate; cook, uncovered, on HIGH (100%) about 2 minutes or until dry, stirring once during cooking.

Poach an egg?
Place 2 teaspoons water in a microwave-safe bowl; cook, uncovered, on HIGH (100%) for 30 seconds. Add egg to bowl, prick egg yolk; cook, covered, on MEDIUM (55%) for 40 seconds or until set. Stand for 30 seconds; drain and invert onto serving plate.

Scramble eggs?
Melt a teaspoon of butter in a microwave-safe bowl; add 2 eggs, whisk until frothy. Cook, uncovered, on HIGH (100%) for 1 1/2 minutes or until just firm, stirring twice during cooking. Stand for 1 minute.

Toast sesame seeds?
To toast 1/4 cup (35g) sesame seeds, place in a microwave-safe bowl; cook, uncovered, on HIGH (100%) about 4 minutes or until browned lightly, stirring twice during cooking.

Soften lumpy sugar?
To soften 1 cup (200g) lumpy, hard brown sugar, place in a microwave-safe bowl with a thick slice of apple on top; cook, covered, on HIGH (100%) about 30 seconds. Stand, covered, 5 minutes before using sugar.

how do I...

Melt marshmallows?
To melt 100g marshmallows, place in a small microwave-safe bowl; cook, uncovered, on HIGH (100%) for about 30 seconds to serve with hot chocolate.

Soften dried fruit?
To soften 1 cup (190g) mixed dried fruit, place in a microwave-safe bowl with 1/4 cup (60ml) water; cook, covered, on HIGH (100%) about 3 minutes or until fruit is soft.

Soften butter or cream cheese?
Place (unwrapped) in a microwave-safe bowl; cook, uncovered, on MEDIUM-LOW (30%) about 10 seconds or until just softened.

Soften ice-cream?
Loosen lid of ice-cream container, place container on turntable; cook, on LOW (10%) about 2 minutes or until soft.

Prepare a jam glaze?
To melt jam to glaze ham, pork or chicken or to brush over pastry tartlets, heat 1/4 cup jam in a small microwave-safe bowl; cook, uncovered, on HIGH (100%) for 1 minute. Strain before using.

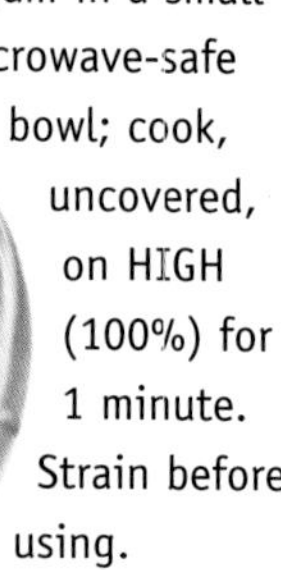

Refresh stale bread rolls or potato chips?
Place 6 bread rolls around the outside of turntable; cook, uncovered, on HIGH (100%) about 30 seconds or until soft. Place 2 cups stale potato chips in a thin layer on 2 sheets of absorbent paper on a microwave-safe plate; cook, uncovered, on HIGH (100%) about 30 seconds. Stand for 5 minutes.

Make porridge for one?
To make 1 serve of porridge, place 1/3 cup rolled oats in microwave-safe bowl with 1 cup (250ml) water. Cook, uncovered, on HIGH (100%) for 2 minutes, stirring once during cooking.

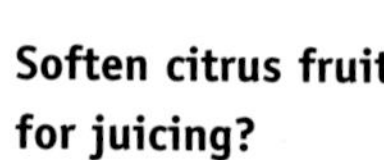

Soften citrus fruit for juicing?
To make citrus fruit squeeze easily, place fruit on turntable; cook; uncovered, on HIGH (100%) for 20 seconds.

Warm plates?
To warm dinner plates for serving, place a damp piece of absorbent paper between each plate in stack of four. Place the four stacked plates on turntable; microwave for 1 minute on HIGH (100%). Remember – plates with a metallic trim are unsuitable for use in a microwave oven.

Steam handtowels?
Roll 4 moistened cloth handtowels and then place on microwave-safe plate; microwave, uncovered, on HIGH (100%) for 1 minute.

Make a white sauce?
Melt 60g butter in a microwave-safe bowl, add 1/4 cup plain flour, mix to a smooth paste. Cook, uncovered, on HIGH (100%) for 1 minute. Gradually whisk in 2 cups milk. Cook, uncovered, on HIGH (100%) for 5 minutes, until sauce boils and thickens, whisking 3 times during cooking.

Make custard?
Blend 1/4 cup custard powder, 2 tablespoons sugar with 1/2 cup milk to form a smooth paste in a microwave-safe bowl. Whisk in 1 1/2 cups of milk; cook, uncovered, on HIGH (100%) for 6 minutes until thick and smooth, stirring 3 times during cooking.

Caramelise onion?
Combine 20g butter and 1 tablespoon brown sugar in a microwave-safe dish; cook, uncovered, on MEDIUM (55%) 30 seconds. Add 1 large onion, sliced thinly; stir until onion is coated with butter and sugar. Cook, uncovered, on HIGH (100%) for 8 minutes, stirring every 2 minutes during cooking.

Cook bacon rashers?
Place 4 rashers bacon on a double layer of absorbent paper on microwave oven turntable. Cover with 2 more layers of absorbent paper. Cook on HIGH (100%) for about 3 minutes or until cooked as desired.

Improve the look of meat cooked in a microwave?
Glaze meat with sauces such as teriyaki, Worcestershire, soy, hoisin and barbecue, or try chutney, marmalade and curry pastes. Dry spices such as paprika, seasoned stale breadcrumbs, seasoned coatings or stock powders may be sprinkled on chicken pieces, hamburger patties and other cut meats.

Cook potatoes?
To cook a medium (250g) potato in its jacket, pierce the potato skin with a fork to allow steam to escape. Cook, uncovered, on microwave oven turntable on HIGH (100%), about 4 minutes or until potato softens.

cooking vegetables

The microwave oven is ideal for cooking vegetables because they retain their colour, flavour and nutrients – and take only minutes to cook! Here's a quick guide on cooking a variety of fresh vegies in your microwave oven.

WING BEANS

ARTICHOKES
QUANTITY: 5 medium (1kg) globe
COOKING PROCEDURE: Trim bases to sit flat, discard tough outer leaves, rinse well. Place artichokes and ¼ cup (60ml) water in large microwave-safe dish; cover.
MICROWAVE TIME ON HIGH (100%): 15 minutes, turning halfway during cooking. Drain upside down; remove hairy choke with a spoon, discard.

ASPARAGUS
QUANTITY: 500g
COOKING PROCEDURE: Snap off woody ends, peel lower part of stem (from spear downward) with vegetable peeler if stems are thick. Place asparagus and 2 tablespoons water in large microwave-safe dish; cover.
MICROWAVE TIME ON HIGH (100%): about 3 minutes or until tender. Drain.

BEANS, SNAKE
QUANTITY: 500g
COOKING PROCEDURE: Cut beans into 10cm lengths. Place snake beans and 1 tablespoon water in large microwave-safe dish; cover.
MICROWAVE TIME ON HIGH (100%): about 5 minutes or until tender, stirring halfway. Stand 1 minute before serving. Drain.

BEANS, GREEN
QUANTITY: 500g
COOKING PROCEDURE: Trim beans as desired. Place green beans and 2 tablespoons water in large microwave-safe dish; cover.
MICROWAVE TIME ON HIGH (100%): about 4 minutes or until tender, stirring halfway. Stand 1 minute before serving. Drain.

BEANS, BUTTER
QUANTITY: 500g
COOKING PROCEDURE: Trim and place butter beans and 2 tablespoons water in large microwave-safe dish; cover.
MICROWAVE TIME ON HIGH (100%): about 4 minutes or until tender, stirring halfway. Stand 1 minute before serving. Drain.

BEANS, BORLOTTI
QUANTITY: 1kg
COOKING PROCEDURE: Shell and place borlotti beans and 2 tablespoons water in large microwave-safe dish; cover.
MICROWAVE TIME ON HIGH (100%): about 15 minutes or until tender, stirring halfway during cooking. Stand 1 minute before serving. Drain.

BEANS, BROAD
QUANTITY: 1kg
COOKING PROCEDURE: Shell and place broad beans and ¼ cup (60ml) water in large microwave-safe bowl; cover.
MICROWAVE TIME ON HIGH (100%): about 6 minutes or until tender, stirring halfway during cooking. Drain then refresh under cold water; drain again.

BEANS, WING
QUANTITY: 500g
COOKING PROCEDURE: Trim and place beans and 1 tablespoon water in large microwave-safe dish; cover.
MICROWAVE TIME ON HIGH (100%): about 5 minutes or until tender, stirring halfway during cooking. Stand 1 minute before serving. Drain.

BEETROOT
QUANTITY: 3 medium (500g), unpeeled, with 3cm of stem remaining
COOKING PROCEDURE: Place beetroot and 2 tablespoons water in large microwave-safe dish; cover.
MICROWAVE TIME ON HIGH (100%): about 30 minutes or until tender, stirring halfway during cooking. Drain, peel while still warm.

BOK CHOY
QUANTITY: 800g
COOKING PROCEDURE: Trim bases of bok choy; separate leaves. Place bok choy and 1 tablespoon water in large microwave-safe dish; cover.
MICROWAVE TIME ON HIGH (100%): about 3 minutes or until tender, stirring halfway during cooking time. Drain.

BROCCOFLOWER
QUANTITY: 500g
COOKING PROCEDURE: Cut broccoflower into florets. Place florets and ¼ cup (60ml) water in large microwave-safe dish; cover.
MICROWAVE TIME ON HIGH (100%): about 3 minutes or until tender, stirring halfway during cooking time. Drain.

BROCCOFLOWER

BROCCOLI
QUANTITY: 500g
COOKING PROCEDURE: Cut broccoli into florets. Place florets and ¼ cup (60ml) water in medium microwave-safe dish; cover.
MICROWAVE TIME ON HIGH (100%): about 5 minutes or until tender, stirring halfway during cooking time. Drain.

BRUSSELS SPROUTS
QUANTITY: 1kg
COOKING PROCEDURE: Cut a cross in base of each sprout; place sprouts and ¼ cup (60ml) water in large microwave-safe dish; cover.
MICROWAVE TIME ON HIGH (100%): about 8 minutes or until tender, stirring halfway during cooking time. Drain.

CABBAGE
QUANTITY: 900g
COOKING PROCEDURE: Chop cabbage coarsely and place with 2 tablespoons water in large microwave-safe dish; cover.
MICROWAVE TIME ON HIGH (100%): about 9 minutes or until tender, stirring halfway during cooking time. Drain.

CARROTS
QUANTITY: 3 large (540g)
COOKING PROCEDURE: Peel and cut into 1cm slices. Place carrots and ¼ cup (60ml) water in large microwave-safe dish; cover.
MICROWAVE TIME ON HIGH (100%): about 8 minutes or until tender, stirring halfway during cooking time. Drain.

CAULIFLOWER
QUANTITY: 500g
COOKING PROCEDURE: Cut cauliflower into florets. Place cauliflower and ¼ cup (60ml) water in large microwave-safe dish; cover.
MICROWAVE TIME ON HIGH (100%): about 6 minutes or until tender, stirring halfway during cooking. Stand 1 minute. Drain.

CELERIAC (sometimes called knob celery)
QUANTITY: 1 large (1.25kg)
COOKING PROCEDURE: Peel and cut celeriac into 2cm pieces. Place celeriac and ¼ cup (60ml) water in large microwave-safe dish; cover.
MICROWAVE TIME ON HIGH (100%): about 20 minutes or until tender, stirring halfway during cooking. Stand 2 minutes. Drain.

CHINESE BROCCOLI
QUANTITY: 900g
COOKING PROCEDURE: Trim and chop Chinese broccoli. Place with 1 tablespoon water in large microwave-safe dish; cover.
MICROWAVE TIME ON HIGH (100%): about 3 minutes or until tender, stirring halfway during cooking time. Drain.

CHOY SU

CHINESE WATER SPINACH

QUANTITY: 175g
COOKING PROCEDURE: Trim bases, separate leaves; chop. Place Chinese water spinach and 1 tablespoon water in large microwave-safe dish; cover.
MICROWAVE TIME ON HIGH (100%): about 3 minutes or until tender, stirring halfway during cooking time. Drain.

CHINESE ZUCCHINI

QUANTITY: 1 medium (1kg)
COOKING PROCEDURE: Remove fuzz with a damp cloth, cut as required. Place Chinese zucchini and 1 tablespoon water in large microwave-safe dish; cover.
MICROWAVE TIME ON HIGH (100%): about 5 minutes or until tender, stirring halfway during cooking time. Drain.

CHOKOES

QUANTITY: 3 large (1kg)
COOKING PROCEDURE: Peel, seed and cut chokoes into 3cm wedges. Place chokoes and ¼ cup (60ml) water in large microwave-safe bowl; cover.
MICROWAVE TIME ON HIGH (100%): about 9 minutes or until tender, stirring halfway during cooking. Stand 2 minutes. Drain.

CHOY SUM

QUANTITY: 1kg
COOKING PROCEDURE: Trim ends, remove open flowers and discard. Place choy sum and 1 tablespoon water in large microwave-safe dish; cover.
MICROWAVE TIME ON HIGH (100%): about 3 minutes or until tender, stirring halfway during cooking time. Drain.

CORN

QUANTITY: 2 medium (600g)
COOKING PROCEDURE: Remove and discard husk and silk. Place corn and 1 tablespoon water in medium microwave-safe dish; cover.
MICROWAVE TIME ON HIGH (100%): about 5 minutes or until tender, turning halfway during cooking time. Drain.

FENNEL

QUANTITY: 2 medium (1.2kg)
COOKING PROCEDURE: Remove stalks and leaves from fennel bulbs, halve lengthways, trim bases to separate halves. Place fennel and ¼ cup (60ml) water in large microwave-safe bowl; cover.
MICROWAVE TIME ON HIGH (100%): 5 minutes or until tender, stirring halfway. Drain.

TAT SOI

KOHLRABI (also known as cabbage turnip)

QUANTITY: 3 medium (1.5kg)
COOKING PROCEDURE: Remove leaves from kohlrabi, peel and chop into 3cm pieces. Place kohlrabi and 2 tablespoons water in large microwave-safe bowl; cover.
MICROWAVE TIME ON HIGH (100%): about 12 minutes or until tender, stirring halfway during cooking time. Drain.

KUMARA

QUANTITY: 2 large (1kg)
COOKING PROCEDURE: Peel and slice into 2cm rounds. Place kumara and 2 tablespoons water in large microwave-safe dish; cover.
MICROWAVE TIME ON HIGH (100%): about 10 minutes or until tender, stirring halfway during cooking time. Drain.

PARSNIPS

QUANTITY: 4 medium (500g)
COOKING PROCEDURE: Peel and chop coarsely. Place parsnips and 2 tablespoons water in large microwave-safe dish; cover.
MICROWAVE TIME ON HIGH (100%): about 6 minutes or until tender, turning halfway during cooking time. Drain.

PEAS, GREEN

QUANTITY: 500g
COOKING PROCEDURE: Shell and place green peas and 1 tablespoon water in large microwave-safe dish; cover.
MICROWAVE TIME ON HIGH (100%): about 3 minutes or until tender, stirring halfway during cooking time. Drain.

PEAS, SUGAR SNAP & SNOW

QUANTITY: 250g of either
COOKING PROCEDURE: Trim ends, remove strings. Place peas and 2 teaspoons water in large microwave-safe dish; cover.
MICROWAVE TIME ON HIGH (100%): about 2 minutes or until tender, stirring halfway during cooking time. Drain.

POTATOES

QUANTITY: 5 medium (1kg)
COOKING PROCEDURE: Peel and quarter. Place potatoes and 2 tablespoons water in large microwave-safe dish; cover.
MICROWAVE TIME ON HIGH (100%): about 10 minutes or until just tender, stirring halfway during cooking time. Drain.

PUMPKIN

QUANTITY: 500g
COOKING PROCEDURE: Peel, seed and chop pumpkin. Place pumpkin and 1 tablespoon water in large microwave-safe dish; cover.
MICROWAVE TIME ON HIGH (100%): about 5 minutes or until tender, stirring halfway during cooking time. Drain.

SILVERBEET

QUANTITY: 500g
COOKING PROCEDURE: Cut off and discard white stems, wash leaves thoroughly. Place whole leaves in large microwave-safe dish; cover.
MICROWAVE TIME ON HIGH (100%): about 4 minutes or until tender, stirring halfway during cooking time. Drain well.

SPINACH (ENGLISH)

QUANTITY: 350g
COOKING PROCEDURE: Cut off and discard roots and about 6cm of lower stems, wash leaves thoroughly. Place spinach in large microwave-safe bowl; cover.
MICROWAVE TIME ON HIGH (100%): about 2 minutes or until just wilted; refresh under cold water. Drain well.

SQUASH

QUANTITY: 500g pattipan
COOKING PROCEDURE: Trim and quarter. Place squash and 2 tablespoons water in medium microwave-safe dish; cover.
MICROWAVE TIME ON HIGH (100%): about 4 minutes or until tender, stirring halfway during cooking time. Drain.

SWEDES

QUANTITY: 4 medium (500g)
COOKING PROCEDURE: Peel swedes thickly and chop into 3cm pieces. Place swedes in large microwave-safe dish; cover.
MICROWAVE TIME ON HIGH (100%): about 8 minutes or until tender, stirring halfway during cooking time. Drain.

TAT SOI AND MUSTARD GREENS

QUANTITY: 300g tat soi or 500g mustard greens
COOKING PROCEDURE: Trim bases, separate leaves. Place tat soi or mustard greens and 1 tablespoon water in large microwave-safe dish; cover.
MICROWAVE TIME ON HIGH (100%): about 3 minutes or until tender, stirring halfway during cooking time. Drain.

TURNIPS

QUANTITY: 4 medium (500g)
COOKING PROCEDURE: Thickly peel and coarsely chop. Place turnips and 1 tablespoon water in large microwave-safe dish; cover.
MICROWAVE TIME ON HIGH (100%): about 6 minutes or until tender, stirring halfway during cooking time. Drain.

ZUCCHINI

QUANTITY: 4 medium (500g)
COOKING PROCEDURE: Trim and halve crossways. Place zucchini and 2 tablespoons water in medium microwave-safe dish; cover.
MICROWAVE TIME ON HIGH (100%): about 5 minutes or until tender, stirring halfway during cooking time. Drain.

KOHLRABI

soups

Whether it's a family meal, lunchtime get-together or formal dinner, nothing is quite as satisfying as a delicious homemade soup. Here are some new takes on old favourites plus a selection of innovative ideas combining the best of Australian fare with a touch of the Orient or sometimes a dash of Europe.

combination short soup

PREPARATION TIME 55 MINUTES • COOKING TIME 20 MINUTES

Ready-to-eat barbecued pork can be purchased from specialty Asian food stores.

1 medium (120g) carrot
2 litres (8 cups) chicken stock
250g spinach, shredded
200g Chinese barbecued pork, sliced
230g can sliced bamboo shoots, rinsed, drained
1/2 cup (40g) bean sprouts
4 green onions, chopped
1 tablespoon soy sauce

PORK AND VEAL POUCHES

150g minced pork and veal
1 green onion, chopped
1 clove garlic, crushed
1 tablespoon oyster sauce
16 gow gee pastry rounds
1 egg white, beaten lightly

1 Cut carrot into 4cm-long thin strips. Bring stock to boil in large microwave-safe bowl, covered, on HIGH (100%) about 10 minutes. Add pork and veal pouches; cook, uncovered, on MEDIUM-HIGH (70%) about 4 minutes or until cooked through.

2 Add carrot and remaining ingredients; cook, uncovered, on MEDIUM-HIGH (70%) 2 minutes.

Pork and veal pouches Combine mince, onion, garlic and sauce in small bowl. Brush each pastry round with egg white, place rounded teaspoons of mince mixture in centre of each round, pinch together to form pouches which enclose filling.

SERVES 6

per serve fat 9.2g; 1183kJ

soaking pulses

Here's a quick way to soak pulses to ready for cooking. Place 1 cup beans or pulses in a microwave-safe bowl, add 2 cups water; cook, covered, on HIGH (100%) for 5 minutes. Stir then cook, covered, on MEDIUM-LOW (30%) a further 30 minutes, stirring occasionally. The beans are now ready to cook in your favourite recipe.

sweet potato soup

PREPARATION TIME 25 MINUTES • COOKING TIME 20 MINUTES

You can use any kind of sweet potato in this recipe; we used kumara, a red-skinned, orange-fleshed variety.

1 teaspoon butter
2 teaspoons vegetable oil
1 medium (150g) brown onion, chopped
1 teaspoon grated fresh ginger
2 cloves garlic, crushed
1/2 teaspoon ground cumin
1/2 teaspoon ground coriander
1 large (500g) kumara, chopped
2 1/2 cups (625ml) chicken stock
1 teaspoon grated orange rind
2 teaspoons tomato paste
2 tablespoons sour cream

1 Combine butter, oil, onion, ginger, garlic and spices in large microwave-safe bowl; cook, uncovered, on HIGH (100%) 4 minutes, stirring once during cooking.

2 Add kumara and 1/2 cup (125ml) of the stock; cook, covered, on HIGH (100%) about 8 minutes or until kumara is tender, stirring once during cooking.

3 Blend or process kumara mixture, remaining stock, rind, paste and cream, in batches, until smooth.

4 Return soup to bowl; cook, covered, on MEDIUM-HIGH (70%) about 3 minutes or until hot, stirring once during cooking. Do not allow soup to boil.

SERVES 4

per serve fat 8.0g; 768kJ

coconutty lentil soup

PREPARATION TIME 25 MINUTES • COOKING TIME 15 MINUTES

30g butter
1 medium (150g) brown onion, chopped finely
1 teaspoon grated fresh ginger
1 clove garlic, crushed
1 birdseye chilli, seeded, chopped finely
1/2 teaspoon ground cardamom
1/2 teaspoon ground turmeric
1 cup (200g) red lentils
3 cups (750ml) chicken stock
1/2 cup (125ml) coconut cream
1 cup (250ml) water, extra
1 tablespoon chopped fresh coriander leaves

1 Combine butter, onion, ginger, garlic, chilli and spices in large microwave-safe bowl; cook, uncovered, on HIGH (100%) about 2 minutes or until onion is soft, stirring once during cooking.

2 Add lentils and stock; cook, covered, on HIGH (100%) about 10 minutes or until lentils are tender, stirring twice during cooking.

3 Stir in cream and extra water; blend or process soup mixture, in batches, until smooth.

4 Return soup to bowl with coriander; cook, uncovered, on MEDIUM (55%) about 3 minutes or until hot.

SERVES 4

per serve fat 13.9g; 1250kJ

indian chowder

PREPARATION TIME 30 MINUTES • COOKING TIME 25 MINUTES

20g butter

1 medium (150g) brown onion, chopped

2 cloves garlic, crushed

3 bacon rashers, chopped

1½ cups (375ml) vegetable stock

2 trimmed (150g) celery sticks, chopped coarsely

1 large (500g) kumara, chopped coarsely

2 tablespoons plain flour

400ml coconut milk

500g spinach, trimmed

nutmeg

1 Combine butter, onion, garlic and bacon in large microwave-safe bowl; cook, uncovered, on HIGH (100%) 5 minutes, stirring once during cooking.

2 Reserve ¼ cup of the stock, add remaining stock to bowl with celery and kumara; cook, covered, on HIGH (100%) about 12 minutes or until vegetables are tender, stirring once during cooking.

3 Add blended flour and reserved stock to bowl with milk; cook, uncovered, on HIGH (100%) about 5 minutes or until chowder boils and thickens slightly, stirring once during cooking.

4 Place spinach in large microwave-safe bowl; cook, covered, on HIGH (100%) about 3 minutes or until wilted. Add spinach to chowder; sprinkle with nutmeg.

SERVES 4

per serve fat 33.8g; 1907kJ

chicken and corn soup

PREPARATION TIME 30 MINUTES • COOKING TIME 10 MINUTES

1.5 litres (6 cups) chicken stock
440g can creamed corn
1 teaspoon sesame oil
1/3 cup (50g) cornflour
1/3 cup (80ml) water
6 green onions, sliced thinly
1/2 teaspoon grated fresh ginger
2 egg whites, beaten lightly
2 tablespoons water, extra
2 slices (45g) ham, sliced thinly
1 cup (170g) shredded cooked chicken
2 teaspoons soy sauce
3 green onions, sliced thinly, extra

1 Heat stock, corn and oil in large microwave-safe bowl, covered, on HIGH (100%) 5 minutes, stirring once during cooking.

2 Stir in blended cornflour and water, then onion and ginger; cook, uncovered, on HIGH (100%) about 5 minutes or until soup boils and thickens slightly, stirring once during cooking.

3 Whisk combined egg white and extra water into hot soup in a thin stream. Stir in ham, chicken and soy; sprinkle with extra onion.

SERVES 6

per serve fat 4.6g; 925kJ

mulligatawny soup

PREPARATION TIME 30 MINUTES • COOKING TIME 25 MINUTES

2 tablespoons Madras curry paste
1 small (200g) leek, sliced
1 trimmed (75g) celery stick, chopped finely
1 medium (120g) carrot, chopped finely
2 cloves garlic, crushed
2 teaspoons grated fresh ginger
1/2 cup (100g) red lentils
1 litre (4 cups) vegetable stock
1 1/2 cups (375ml) coconut milk
1 medium (150g) apple, peeled, grated
250g cooked roast beef, sliced
2 tablespoons lime juice
2 tablespoons chopped fresh coriander leaves

1 Combine paste, leek, celery, carrot, garlic and ginger in large microwave-safe bowl; cook, covered, on HIGH (100%) 4 minutes, stirring once during cooking.

2 Add lentils and stock; cook, covered, on HIGH (100%) 15 minutes, stirring once during cooking. Blend or process mixture, in batches, until smooth; return to bowl.

3 Add milk, apple and beef; cook soup, covered, on MEDIUM-HIGH (70%) 5 minutes. Stir in juice and coriander.

SERVES 6

per serve fat 22.5g; 1418kJ

chicken minestrone

PREPARATION TIME 25 MINUTES • COOKING TIME 25 MINUTES

500g chicken thigh fillets, chopped
1 medium (150g) brown onion, sliced
1 clove garlic, crushed
2 bacon rashers, chopped
1 trimmed (75g) celery stick, chopped
1 medium (120g) carrot, chopped coarsely
400g can tomatoes
300g can kidney beans, rinsed, drained
3 cups (750ml) chicken stock
40g macaroni
2 tablespoons chopped fresh oregano
1 tablespoon chopped fresh parsley

1 Combine chicken, onion, garlic, bacon, celery and carrot in large microwave-safe bowl; cook, covered, on MEDIUM-HIGH (70%) 15 minutes, stirring once during cooking.

2 Add undrained crushed tomatoes, beans, stock and pasta; cook, uncovered, on MEDIUM-HIGH (70%) about 10 minutes or until pasta is just tender. Stir in herbs.

SERVES 4

per serve fat 10.3g; 1526kJ

spicy pumpkin soup with tortellini

PREPARATION TIME 30 MINUTES
COOKING TIME 25 MINUTES

250g beef tortellini
2 cups (500ml) boiling water
2 tablespoons olive oil
1 medium (150g) brown onion, chopped finely
1 clove garlic, crushed
1/2 teaspoon ground coriander
1 teaspoon ground cumin
1kg pumpkin, chopped
1 medium (200g) potato, chopped
1 litre (4 cups) chicken stock
1/2 cup (125ml) cream
1 tablespoon chopped fresh chives
1 tablespoon chopped fresh basil leaves

1. Combine pasta with boiling water in medium microwave-safe bowl; cook, uncovered, on HIGH (100%) about 3 minutes or until tender, stirring once during cooking. Drain.
2. Combine oil, onion, garlic, coriander and cumin in large microwave-safe bowl; cook, uncovered, on HIGH (100%) 2 minutes, stirring once during cooking.
3. Stir in pumpkin, potato and stock; cook, covered, on HIGH (100%) about 10 minutes or until pumpkin is tender, stirring once during cooking. Stand 5 minutes.
4. Blend or process mixture, in batches, until smooth. Return soup to bowl with cream, herbs and pasta; cook, uncovered, on HIGH (100%) about 2 minutes or until heated through.

SERVES 6

per serve fat 17.5g; 1609kJ

hearty vegetable soup with pesto

PREPARATION TIME 40 MINUTES
COOKING TIME 15 MINUTES

30g butter
1 medium (120g) carrot, chopped coarsely
1 medium (200g) potato, chopped coarsely
60g green beans, chopped coarsely
1 medium (120g) zucchini, chopped coarsely
1 medium (150g) brown onion, chopped finely
400g can tomatoes
2 tablespoons plain flour
2 tablespoons tomato paste
3 cups (750ml) vegetable stock
2 teaspoons sugar
300g can butter beans, rinsed, drained

PESTO

1 cup firmly packed fresh basil leaves
250g spinach, trimmed
1/2 cup (40g) grated parmesan cheese
1/2 cup (80g) pine nuts
5 cloves garlic, quartered
1/2 cup (125ml) olive oil

1. Combine butter, fresh vegetables and undrained crushed tomatoes in large microwave-safe bowl; cook, covered, on HIGH (100%) 10 minutes.
2. Whisk in flour, paste, stock and sugar; cook, covered, on HIGH (100%) about 5 minutes or until vegetables are soft and soup boils and thickens, stirring twice during cooking.
3. Stir in butter beans. Serve soup topped with pesto.

Pesto Blend or process basil, spinach, cheese, nuts and garlic until smooth, adding oil gradually in a thin stream while motor is operating.

SERVES 4

per serve fat 55.2g; 2734kJ

hearty vegetable soup with pesto *(front)*
spicy pumpkin soup with tortellini *(back)*

main meals

Need a nourishing meal for the family or entertaining unexpected guests in a hurry? You'll never be stuck for ideas again! And the beauty of using your microwave oven is the simplicity and speed with which you can produce delectable meals from these foolproof recipes, just right for busy people.

chicken with lemon mustard sauce

PREPARATION TIME 25 MINUTES • COOKING TIME 20 MINUTES

30g butter
1 tablespoon vegetable oil
1 medium (150g) brown onion, sliced
1 clove garlic, crushed
4 single (680g) chicken breast fillets
2 teaspoons sweet paprika
300ml cream
1 teaspoon finely grated lemon rind
2 teaspoons lemon juice
2 teaspoons seeded mustard
1 chicken stock cube
2 teaspoons cornflour
1 tablespoon water
2 tablespoons finely chopped fresh chives

1 Combine butter, oil, onion and garlic in large shallow microwave-safe dish; cook, uncovered, on HIGH (100%) 4 minutes, stirring once during cooking. Remove onion mixture from dish.

2 Place chicken in same dish; sprinkle with paprika. Cook, covered, on MEDIUM-HIGH (70%) about 10 minutes or until cooked through. Remove chicken from dish; cover to keep warm.

3 Return onion mixture to same dish with cream, rind, juice, mustard, crumbled stock cube and blended cornflour and the water; cook, uncovered, on HIGH (100%) about 3 minutes or until sauce boils and thickens slightly, stirring once during cooking. Stir chives through sauce; serve with chicken.

SERVES 4

serve with green beans or broccoli and pinenuts, page 78
per serve 47.5g fat; 2563kJ

cooking bacon

Here's a quick and easy way to crisp bacon for use in a recipe. Chop 3 rashers of bacon finely, place on a microwave-safe plate between double thicknesses of absorbent paper then cook on HIGH (100%) for 3 minutes. Just right to sprinkle on top of baked potatoes or a casserole.

curried vegetable and bacon patties

PREPARATION TIME 30 MINUTES (PLUS CHILLING TIME) • COOKING TIME 25 MINUTES

4 medium (800g) potatoes, chopped coarsely
2 tablespoons water
30g butter
2 tablespoons cream
1 egg yolk
6 bacon rashers, chopped
1 small (80g) brown onion, chopped finely
1 clove garlic, crushed
1 tablespoon mild curry powder
2 cups (160g) shredded cabbage
1 medium (120g) carrot, grated coarsely
3 cups (210g) stale breadcrumbs
1/2 cup (75g) Corn Flake Crumbs

1 Combine potato with the water in large microwave-safe bowl; cook, covered, on HIGH (100%) about 10 minutes or until tender; drain.

2 Mash potato, butter, cream and yolk together in same bowl.

3 Combine bacon, onion and garlic in large microwave-safe bowl; cook, covered, on HIGH (100%) 4 minutes, stirring once during cooking.

4 Stir in curry powder and vegetables; cook, covered, on HIGH (100%) 2 minutes. Stir in potato mixture and stale breadcrumbs, cover; refrigerate 1 hour.

5 Shape mixture into 8 patties, press Corn Flake Crumbs all over patties. Place patties around edge of microwave oven turntable; cook, uncovered, on HIGH (100%) 5 minutes.

SERVES 4

serve with a salad of mixed cresses and tomato wedges
per serve 24.6g fat; 2443kJ

creamy beef stroganoff

PREPARATION TIME 25 MINUTES • COOKING TIME 25 MINUTES

60g butter
1 medium (150g) brown onion, sliced
2 cloves garlic, crushed
1 teaspoon sweet paprika
250g button mushrooms, sliced
500g beef fillet steak, sliced thinly
2 tablespoons plain flour
1 cup (250ml) beef stock
1 tablespoon dry sherry
2 tablespoons tomato paste
1 teaspoon Worcestershire sauce
1/2 cup (125ml) sour cream
1 tablespoon chopped fresh chives

1 Combine butter, onion, garlic and paprika in large microwave-safe bowl; cook, uncovered, on HIGH (100%) 4 minutes, stirring once during cooking.

2 Add mushrooms; cook, uncovered, on HIGH (100%) 2 minutes. Coat beef with flour, add to mushroom mixture; cook, uncovered, on MEDIUM-HIGH (70%) 2 minutes.

3 Add stock, sherry, paste and sauce; cook, uncovered, on MEDIUM-HIGH (70%) about 15 minutes or until beef is tender and mixture thickens slightly, stirring twice during cooking. Stir in sour cream and chives.

SERVES 4

serve with noodles or rice and steamed greens
per serve 32.7g fat; 1962kJ

chickpea and vegetable stuffed capsicums

PREPARATION TIME 20 MINUTES • COOKING TIME 30 MINUTES

3 medium (600g) red capsicums
2 medium (240g) zucchini, chopped finely
1 small (80g) brown onion, sliced thinly
100g green beans, chopped
300g can chickpeas, rinsed, drained
1 tablespoon olive oil
1/2 cup (40g) flaked parmesan cheese

TOMATO SAUCE

2 x 400g cans tomatoes
1 tablespoon balsamic vinegar
1/2 teaspoon sugar
1/4 cup shredded fresh basil leaves

1 Halve capsicums lengthways, remove seeds and membranes. Place capsicum halves, cut-side up, in 3-litre (12-cup) shallow microwave-safe dish.

2 Spoon combined zucchini, onion, beans, chickpeas and oil into capsicum halves; pour over tomato sauce. Cook, covered, on HIGH (100%) about 20 minutes or until vegetables are tender. Serve topped with cheese.

Tomato sauce Combine undrained crushed tomatoes, vinegar and sugar in large microwave-safe bowl; cook, uncovered, on HIGH (100%) 8 minutes, stirring once during cooking. Stir in basil.

SERVES 6

serve with green salad or stir-fried Asian greens
per serve 6.5g fat; 609kJ

potato frittata

PREPARATION TIME 30 MINUTES • COOKING TIME 35 MINUTES

2 teaspoons vegetable oil
1 large (200g) brown onion, sliced thinly
1 clove garlic, crushed
1 small (150g) red capsicum, chopped finely
130g can corn kernels, drained
2 teaspoons chopped fresh oregano
2 medium (400g) potatoes, sliced thinly
6 eggs, beaten lightly
1/2 cup (125ml) milk
2 teaspoons chopped fresh thyme
1/2 cup (60g) coarsely grated cheddar cheese

1 Grease 20cm-square 2-litre (8-cup) microwave-safe dish; line base with baking paper, extending paper 2cm above two opposite sides of dish.

2 Combine oil, onion, garlic and capsicum in medium microwave-safe bowl; cook, covered, on HIGH (100%) 3 minutes, stirring once during cooking. Drain on absorbent paper; combine onion mixture with corn and oregano in same bowl.

3 Layer half the potato over base of prepared dish, top with onion mixture then remaining potato. Pour over combined eggs and milk; cook, uncovered, on MEDIUM (55%) about 20 minutes or until centre is almost set.

4 Sprinkle with thyme and cheese; cook, uncovered, on MEDIUM (55%) about 8 minutes or until cheese melts and frittata is just set. Stand, covered, 5 minutes.

SERVES 4

serve with a tossed salad of fennel and rocket
per serve 17.7g fat; 1323kJ

beef and nut biryani

PREPARATION TIME 30 MINUTES (PLUS CHILLING AND STANDING TIME) • COOKING TIME 35 MINUTES

500g beef fillet steak, sliced thinly
2 teaspoons sambal oelek
2 teaspoons ground coriander
1 teaspoon ground cumin
1 teaspoon ground turmeric
1 tablespoon white vinegar
1/3 cup (80ml) yogurt
2 cups (400g) white long-grain rice
50g ghee
2 large (400g) brown onions, chopped finely
2 cups (500ml) hot beef stock
1 cup (125g) frozen peas, thawed
2 medium (380g) tomatoes, chopped coarsely
2 tablespoons chopped fresh coriander leaves
3/4 cup (105g) slivered almonds

1 Combine beef with sambal, ground spices, vinegar and yogurt in medium bowl, cover; refrigerate 30 minutes.

2 Place rice in medium bowl, cover with water; stand 30 minutes, drain.

3 Combine ghee and onion in large microwave-safe bowl; cook, covered, on HIGH (100%) 6 minutes, stirring once during cooking.

4 Add beef mixture, rice and stock to onion mixture; cook, covered, on MEDIUM-HIGH (70%) about 20 minutes or until rice is tender and beef cooked through, stirring once during cooking.

5 Stir peas, tomato and fresh coriander into rice mixture, cover; stand 5 minutes.

6 Meanwhile, cook nuts on microwave-safe plate, uncovered, on HIGH (100%) about 3 minutes or until browned lightly, stirring twice during cooking. Stir into biryani.

SERVES 4

serve with dried fruit chutney, page 113

per serve 36.5g fat; 3691kJ

mustard lamb racks with sun-dried tomato crust

PREPARATION TIME 15 MINUTES • COOKING TIME 25 MINUTES

4 racks of lamb with 4 cutlets each
1 tablespoon Dijon mustard
1 cup (70g) stale breadcrumbs
2 cloves garlic, crushed
1/4 cup (35g) drained finely chopped sun-dried tomatoes in oil
1 egg white, beaten lightly

FRESH THYME SAUCE

3 teaspoons cornflour
1 tablespoon water
1/2 cup (125ml) beef stock
1 tablespoon dry red wine
1/2 cup (125ml) tomato juice
1 tablespoon drained finely chopped sun-dried tomatoes in oil
1 teaspoon chopped fresh thyme

1 Spread backs of lamb racks with mustard. Combine breadcrumbs, garlic, tomato and egg white in small bowl, press onto mustard.

2 Place lamb racks, crust-side up, with meaty ends towards edge of large shallow microwave-safe dish; cook, uncovered, on MEDIUM-HIGH (70%) about 12 minutes or until almost cooked as desired. Stand, covered, 10 minutes. Serve with fresh thyme sauce.

Fresh thyme sauce Blend cornflour with the water in microwave-safe jug, stir in stock, wine and juice; cook, uncovered, on HIGH (100%) about 3 minutes or until sauce boils and thickens slightly, whisking once during cooking. Stir in tomato and thyme.

SERVES 4

serve with cauliflower au gratin, page 75, and steamed greens
per serve 30g fat; 1995kJ

creamy broccoli and bacon pasta

PREPARATION TIME 20 MINUTES • COOKING TIME 15 MINUTES

500g fresh fettuccine
1.5 litres (6 cups) boiling water
30g butter
1 small (80g) brown onion, chopped
2 bacon rashers, chopped
1 clove garlic, crushed
250g broccoli, chopped finely
2 teaspoons cornflour
1 tablespoon water, extra
1 chicken stock cube
300ml cream
2 tablespoons finely grated parmesan cheese

1 Combine pasta with the boiling water in large microwave-safe bowl; cook, uncovered, on HIGH (100%) about 5 minutes or until pasta is tender, stirring once during cooking. Drain pasta; cover to keep warm.

2 Combine butter, onion, bacon and garlic in large microwave-safe bowl; cook, uncovered, on HIGH (100%) 4 minutes, stirring once during cooking. Add broccoli; cook, covered, on HIGH (100%) 2 minutes.

3 Stir in blended cornflour and the extra water, crumbled stock cube, cream and cheese; cook, uncovered, on HIGH (100%) about 3 minutes or until sauce boils and thickens slightly, stirring once during cooking. Toss pasta through hot sauce.

SERVES 4

serve with crusty Italian bread
per serve 47g fat; 3471kJ

florentine chicken mozzarella

PREPARATION TIME 15 MINUTES • COOKING TIME 20 MINUTES

Cream ceramic platter from Empire Homewares

250g frozen spinach, thawed
4 single (680g) chicken breast fillets
1 tablespoon olive oil
120g mozzarella cheese, sliced thinly
2¹/₃ cups (600ml) bottled chunky tomato pasta sauce
1 tablespoon chopped fresh basil leaves

1 Drain spinach then, using hand, squeeze out excess liquid; chop spinach coarsely.

2 Brush chicken with oil and place in large shallow microwave-safe dish; cook, covered, on MEDIUM-HIGH (70%) about 8 minutes or until almost cooked through. Drain away liquid.

3 Top chicken with spinach then cheese. Pour combined sauce and basil into dish; cook, uncovered, on MEDIUM (55%) about 8 minutes or until cheese melts and sauce is hot.

SERVES 4

serve with baby potatoes tossed in chive butter and baby beans
per serve 16.7g fat; 1759kJ

home-style meatloaf

PREPARATION TIME 15 MINUTES • COOKING TIME 45 MINUTES

1 tablespoon olive oil
1 medium (150g) brown onion, chopped
1 small (150g) red capsicum, chopped
500g minced beef
250g sausage mince
1 cup (70g) stale breadcrumbs
1 egg
2 tablespoons tomato paste
2 teaspoons chopped fresh oregano
1 tablespoon tomato sauce
2 teaspoons soy sauce
2 teaspoons brown sugar

1 Combine oil, onion and capsicum in medium microwave-safe bowl; cook, covered, on HIGH (100%) 4 minutes, stirring once during cooking.

2 Add minces, breadcrumbs, egg, paste and oregano to same bowl, mix well.

3 Shape mixture into a 10cm x 25cm loaf on microwave oven turntable. Brush with combined sauces and sugar; cook, uncovered, on MEDIUM (55%) about 30 minutes or until firm. Stand, covered, 10 minutes.

SERVES 6

serve with creamy potato mash or crusty bread
per serve 24.1g fat; 1498kJ

thai-style chicken curry

PREPARATION TIME 20 MINUTES • COOKING TIME 15 MINUTES

1 tablespoon vegetable oil
1 tablespoon Thai red curry paste
500g chicken thigh fillets, sliced thickly
$^2/_3$ cup (160ml) coconut milk
1 tablespoon fish sauce
4 green onions, sliced thinly
230g can sliced bamboo shoots, rinsed, drained
1 tablespoon coarsely chopped fresh basil leaves

1 Combine oil and paste in large microwave-safe bowl; cook, covered, on HIGH (100%) about 1 minute or until fragrant.

2 Add chicken; cook, covered, on MEDIUM-HIGH (70%) about 8 minutes or until cooked through, gently stirring once during cooking.

3 Add milk, sauce, onion and bamboo shoots; cook, uncovered, on MEDIUM (55%) about 4 minutes or until heated through. Stir in basil.

SERVES 4

serve with steamed jasmine rice and bok choy with mushrooms, page 71
per serve 20.8g fat; 1330kJ

risotto marinara

PREPARATION TIME 30 MINUTES • COOKING TIME 30 MINUTES

30 (750g) medium uncooked prawns
2 tablespoons olive oil
1 medium (150g) brown onion, chopped finely
2 cups (400g) arborio rice
3½ cups (875ml) hot vegetable stock
500g seafood marinara mix
½ cup (125ml) cream
½ cup (40g) coarsely grated parmesan cheese
¼ cup chopped fresh parsley

1 Shell and devein prawns, cut in half lengthways.

2 Combine oil and onion in large microwave-safe bowl; cook, uncovered, on HIGH (100%) 4 minutes, stirring once during cooking. Stir in rice; cook, uncovered, on HIGH (100%) 1 minute.

3 Add stock; cook, covered, on HIGH (100%) 10 minutes, stirring twice during cooking.

4 Stir in all seafood; cook, covered, on MEDIUM (55%) about 6 minutes or until seafood has changed in colour and rice is just tender, stirring once during cooking.

5 Stir in cream and cheese; cook, covered, on MEDIUM (55%) 3 minutes. Stand, covered, 5 minutes; stir in parsley.

SERVES 4

serve with a green leaf salad
per serve 30.2g fat; 3437kJ

Cream ceramic plates from Empire Homewares; glass bottle from The Bay Tree Kitchen Shop

pork with caramelised apples

PREPARATION TIME 20 MINUTES • COOKING TIME 30 MINUTES

800g pork fillets
2 teaspoons cornflour
1 tablespoon water
1/3 cup (80ml) orange juice
1/4 cup (60ml) chicken stock
2 tablespoons port
2 tablespoons blackberry jam
20g butter
2 medium (300g) red apples, sliced
2 tablespoons brown sugar

1 Cook pork in large shallow microwave-safe dish, uncovered, on MEDIUM (55%) 5 minutes; drain. Turn pork; cook, uncovered, on MEDIUM (55%) 5 minutes. Repeat once more or until pork is almost tender; cover, stand 5 minutes.

2 Blend cornflour with water in microwave-safe jug, stir in juice, stock, port and jam; cook, uncovered, on HIGH (100%) for about 2 minutes or until sauce boils and thickens, whisking once during cooking.

3 Melt butter in large shallow microwave-safe dish, uncovered, on HIGH (100%) 30 seconds. Stir in apple and sugar, cook, uncovered, on HIGH (100%) about 5 minutes or until apples are soft, stirring once during cooking. Serve pork with apples and sauce.

SERVES 6

serve with fresh steamed asparagus and snow peas
per serve 4.9g fat; 1043kJ

tasty coated chicken

PREPARATION TIME 25 MINUTES (PLUS CHILLING TIME) • COOKING TIME 20 MINUTES

8 (1.3kg) chicken thigh cutlets
2 tablespoons plain flour
2 tablespoons chicken stock powder
1/2 teaspoon five-spice powder
1 teaspoon garlic salt
1 teaspoon celery salt
1 egg
2 tablespoons milk
3/4 cup (75g) Corn Flake Crumbs
60g butter

1 Discard chicken skin. Toss chicken in combined flour, powders and salts; shake away excess. Dip chicken into combined egg and milk, then coat in crumbs. Cover; refrigerate 1 hour.

2 Melt butter in small microwave-safe bowl, uncovered, on HIGH (100%) 1 minute.

3 Cover microwave oven turntable with 2 layers of absorbent paper; place chicken in single layer on paper. Brush chicken lightly with butter, cover with 2 layers of absorbent paper. Cook on MEDIUM-HIGH (70%) 8 minutes.

4 Rotate chicken pieces, re-cover with paper; cook on MEDIUM-HIGH (70%) about 8 minutes or until cooked through.

SERVES 4

serve with butter beans, sugar snap peas and a dipping sauce of soy and chilli
per serve 26.1g fat; 3184kJ

spiced apricot and chicken tagine

PREPARATION TIME 25 MINUTES • COOKING TIME 30 MINUTES

1 tablespoon olive oil
1kg chicken thigh fillets, chopped
2 cloves garlic, crushed
1 large (200g) brown onion, chopped finely
1/4 teaspoon ground cinnamon
1/2 teaspoon ground cumin
1/2 teaspoon ground ginger
1/2 teaspoon ground turmeric
1 cup (250ml) hot chicken stock
1 tablespoon honey
1 cup (150g) dried apricots
1 tablespoon cornflour
1 tablespoon water
1/2 cup (80g) blanched almonds
2 tablespoons chopped fresh coriander leaves

1 Combine oil, chicken, garlic, onion and spices in large microwave-safe bowl; cook, covered, on MEDIUM-HIGH (70%) 15 minutes, stirring once during cooking.

2 Add stock, honey and apricots; cook, uncovered, on MEDIUM-HIGH (70%) about 5 minutes or until apricots are tender. Stir in blended cornflour and the water; cook, uncovered, on MEDIUM-HIGH (70%) about 3 minutes or until mixture boils and thickens slightly, whisking once during cooking.

3 Cook nuts on microwave-safe plate, uncovered, on HIGH (100%) about 3 minutes or until browned lightly, stirring twice during cooking. Stir nuts and coriander into tagine.

SERVES 4

serve with couscous
per serve 26.8g fat; 2450kJ

coq au vin

PREPARATION TIME 25 MINUTES • COOKING TIME 30 MINUTES

20g butter
8 (880g) chicken thigh fillets, halved
2 cloves garlic, crushed
3 bacon rashers, chopped
10 (250g) spring onions, trimmed
200g Swiss brown mushrooms, halved
2 tablespoons brandy
1/2 cup (125ml) dry red wine
1/2 cup (125ml) chicken stock
1 sprig fresh parsley
2 teaspoons chopped fresh thyme
1 bay leaf
2 tablespoons tomato paste
2 tablespoons cornflour
2 tablespoons water

1 Combine butter, chicken, garlic, bacon and onions in 3-litre (12-cup) shallow microwave-safe dish; cook, covered, on MEDIUM-HIGH (70%) 15 minutes, stirring once during cooking.

2 Stir in mushrooms, brandy, wine, stock, herbs, bay leaf and paste; cook, covered, on MEDIUM-HIGH (70%) about 10 minutes or until chicken is very tender, stirring once during cooking.

3 Stir blended cornflour blended and the water into mixture in dish; cook, uncovered, on MEDIUM-HIGH (70%) about 2 minutes or until mixture boils and thickens slightly.

SERVES 6

serve with creamy mashed potatoes and steamed vegetables
per serve 12.7g fat; 1307kJ

chicken, bean and sausage casserole

PREPARATION TIME 30 MINUTES • COOKING TIME 40 MINUTES

3 bacon rashers, sliced
2 thin (165g) spicy Italian sausages
2 thin (100g) beef sausages
9 (1kg) chicken thigh fillets, halved
2 cloves garlic, crushed
3 cloves
12 black peppercorns
1 trimmed (75g) stick celery, sliced
4 medium (480g) carrots, sliced
2 medium (300g) onions, sliced
300g can butter beans, rinsed, drained
1/2 cup (125ml) dry white wine
1/2 cup (125ml) chicken stock
2 tablespoons tomato paste

1 Cook bacon between double thicknesses of absorbent paper, on HIGH (100%) about 5 minutes or until crisp. Drain on absorbent paper; reserve.

2 Prick sausages with fork, place in 3-litre (12-cup) shallow microwave-safe dish, cover with sheet of absorbent paper; cook on MEDIUM-HIGH (70%) about 5 minutes or until cooked through. Cool sausages; slice thickly.

3 Add chicken to same dish; cook, covered, on MEDIUM-HIGH (70%) 10 minutes, stirring once during cooking.

4 Add garlic, cloves, peppercorns, celery, carrot, onion, beans, wine, stock and paste; cook, covered, on MEDIUM-HIGH (70%) about 20 minutes or until chicken and vegetables are very tender, stirring once during cooking. Stir in sausage; serve casserole sprinkled with bacon.

SERVES 6

serve with steamed rice or couscous
per serve 20.6g fat; 1753kJ

chilli chicken and salami casserole

PREPARATION TIME 20 MINUTES • COOKING TIME 35 MINUTES

250g csabai salami, sliced
1 tablespoon olive oil
9 (1.5kg) chicken thigh cutlets
1 large (300g) red onion, sliced
4 cloves garlic, crushed
2 teaspoons ground cumin
2 teaspoons sweet paprika
3 large (750g) tomatoes, chopped
1/2 cup (125ml) chicken stock
2 tablespoons chilli sauce
2 tablespoons chopped fresh oregano
2 tablespoons lemon juice

1. Cook salami between double thicknesses of absorbent paper on HIGH (100%) about 3 minutes or until crisp.
2. Combine oil, chicken, onion, garlic and spices in 3-litre (12-cup) shallow microwave-safe dish; cook, covered, on MEDIUM-HIGH (70%) 10 minutes, turning chicken pieces once during cooking.
3. Add salami, tomato, stock, sauce, oregano and juice; cook, covered, on MEDIUM-HIGH (70%) 20 minutes, turning chicken pieces once during cooking.

SERVES 6

serve with jacket potatoes
per serve 34.5g fat; 2097kJ

pasta carbonara

PREPARATION TIME 15 MINUTES
COOKING TIME 25 MINUTES

500g fettuccine
2 litres (8 cups) boiling water
1 teaspoon olive oil
6 bacon rashers, sliced thinly
300ml cream
4 eggs, beaten lightly
1 cup (80g) finely grated parmesan cheese

1 Break pasta in half. Combine pasta, boiling water and oil in large microwave-safe bowl; cook, uncovered, on HIGH (100%) about 12 minutes or until just tender, stirring twice during cooking. Drain pasta; cover to keep warm.

2 Place bacon in large microwave-safe bowl, cover with sheet of absorbent paper; cook on HIGH (100%) about 6 minutes or until crisp, stirring once during cooking. Discard absorbent paper. Add cream to bowl; cook, uncovered, on HIGH (100%) 4 minutes.

3 Working quickly, gently mix hot pasta and combined eggs and cheese with bacon mixture in bowl. Cook, uncovered, on MEDIUM (55%) about 2 minutes or until hot, mixing gently once during cooking.

SERVES 4

serve with fresh loaf of warm ciabatta
per serve 57.1g fat; 4321kJ

curried chickpeas and rice

PREPARATION TIME 15 MINUTES • COOKING TIME 45 MINUTES

2/3 cup (130g) brown long-grain rice
1.5 litres (6 cups) boiling water
2 tablespoons mild curry paste
2 medium (300g) brown onions, chopped finely
2 cloves garlic, crushed
2 x 425g cans chickpeas, rinsed, drained
1 1/2 cups (375ml) hot chicken stock
1 tablespoon mango chutney
1 cup (250ml) coconut cream
1/4 cup finely chopped fresh coriander leaves

1 Combine rice with the boiling water in large microwave-safe bowl; cook uncovered, on HIGH (100%) about 25 minutes or until tender. Drain.
2 Combine paste, onion and garlic in large microwave-safe bowl; cook, covered, on HIGH (100%) 5 minutes, stirring once during cooking. Add chickpeas and stock; cook, covered, on HIGH (100%) 10 minutes.
3 Stir in chutney, cream and rice; cook, uncovered, on HIGH (100%) 5 minutes. Stir in fresh coriander leaves.

SERVES 4

serve with chopped cucumber and yogurt or chopped tomato and onion
per serve 21.3g fat; 1896kJ

chilli garlic lamb with noodles

PREPARATION TIME 25 MINUTES (PLUS MARINATING TIME) • COOKING TIME 20 MINUTES

500g lamb fillets, sliced
2 tablespoons mild chilli sauce
2 tablespoons hoisin sauce
2 tablespoons sweet sherry
2 cloves garlic, crushed
500g thick fresh egg noodles
2 tablespoons peanut oil
1 bunch Chinese broccoli, chopped coarsely
2 tablespoons soy sauce
2 teaspoons smooth peanut butter
2 teaspoons cornflour
1/2 cup (125ml) water

Forks and glass from Empire Homewares

1 Combine lamb with chilli and hoisin sauce, sherry and garlic in large microwave-safe bowl, cover; refrigerate 3 hours or overnight.

2 Rinse noodles in hot water to separate; drain.

3 Stir oil into undrained lamb mixture; cook, uncovered, on MEDIUM-HIGH (70%) 8 minutes, stirring once during cooking.

4 Add broccoli, soy sauce, peanut butter and blended cornflour and the water; cook, uncovered, on MEDIUM-HIGH (70%) about 4 minutes or until mixture boils and thickens slightly.

5 Toss noodles through lamb mixture; cook, uncovered, on MEDIUM-HIGH (70%) about 3 minutes or until hot.

SERVES 4

serve with combination short soup, page 16, to start the meal
per serve 23.1g fat; 2177kJ

vegetable and split pea curry

PREPARATION TIME 25 MINUTES (PLUS SOAKING TIME) • COOKING TIME 40 MINUTES

1 cup (200g) green split peas
1 tablespoon peanut oil
1 large (200g) brown onion, sliced
1 tablespoon mild curry powder
2 teaspoons ground ginger
2 teaspoons ground cumin
2 teaspoons ground coriander
1 teaspoon ground turmeric
400g can tomatoes
3/4 cup (180ml) vegetable stock
1 cup (250ml) coconut milk
10 (400g) tiny new potatoes, quartered
1 medium (400g) kumara, chopped
2 medium (240g) carrots, chopped
4 medium (480g) zucchini, chopped
1 tablespoon chopped fresh coriander leaves
1 tablespoon lime juice

1 Place peas in medium bowl, cover with cold water, soak 1 hour; drain.

2 Combine oil, onion, powder and ground spices in 3-litre (12-cup) shallow microwave-safe dish; cook, covered, on HIGH (100%) 5 minutes, stirring gently once during cooking.

3 Add peas, undrained crushed tomatoes and stock; cook, covered, on HIGH (100%) 15 minutes.

4 Add milk and vegetables; cook, covered, on HIGH (100%) about 20 minutes or until vegetables and peas are tender, stirring gently twice during cooking. Stir in fresh coriander and juice.

SERVES 6

serve with warm naan or pappadams
per serve 14.8g fat; 1486kJ

singapore noodles

PREPARATION TIME 35 MINUTES (PLUS STANDING TIME) • COOKING TIME 15 MINUTES

10 dried shiitake mushrooms
450g thin fresh egg noodles
16 (400g) medium uncooked prawns
2 tablespoons peanut oil
5 cloves garlic, crushed
1 tablespoon grated fresh ginger
2 tablespoons mild curry paste
230g can water chestnuts, drained, chopped
4 green onions, chopped
200g Chinese barbecued pork, sliced
2 tablespoons soy sauce
2 tablespoons oyster sauce
2 tablespoons dry sherry
3 eggs, beaten lightly
2 teaspoons sesame oil

1 Place mushrooms in small heatproof bowl, cover with boiling water, stand 20 minutes; drain. Discard stems; chop mushroom caps finely.

2 Rinse noodles under cold water; drain. Shell and devein prawns, leaving tails intact.

3 Combine oil, garlic, ginger and paste in large microwave-safe bowl; cook, covered, on HIGH (100%) 1 minute. Add mushrooms, chestnuts, onion and pork; cook, uncovered, on MEDIUM-HIGH (70%) 2 minutes.

4 Add prawns; cook, uncovered, on MEDIUM (55%) about 5 minutes or until prawns just change in colour. Add noodles, combined sauces and sherry; cook, uncovered, on MEDIUM (55%) 4 minutes, stirring once during cooking.

5 Add combined eggs and sesame oil; mix gently. Cook, uncovered, on MEDIUM (55%) about 3 minutes or until eggs are just cooked, stirring gently once during cooking.

SERVES 4

Serve with combination short soup, page 16, or chicken and corn soup, page 21, as a first course
per serve 30g fat; 2419kJ

Steel bowls from Empire Homewares

risotto primavera

PREPARATION TIME 15 MINUTES • COOKING TIME 25 MINUTES

250g fresh asparagus, trimmed, chopped
2 tablespoons olive oil
1½ cups (300g) arborio rice
1 clove garlic, crushed
1 litre (4 cups) hot chicken stock
1 cup (125g) frozen peas
¼ cup (60ml) cream
2 teaspoons Dijon mustard
⅓ cup (25g) coarsely grated parmesan cheese
2 tablespoons finely chopped fresh mint leaves

1 Cook asparagus in large microwave-safe bowl, covered, on HIGH (100%) 1 minute. Rinse asparagus under cold water; drain.

2 Combine oil, rice and garlic in same bowl; cook, covered, on HIGH (100%) 1 minute. Add 2 cups (500ml) of the stock; cook, covered, on HIGH (100%) 5 minutes. Stir then add remaining stock; cook, covered, on HIGH (100%) 5 minutes, stirring once during cooking.

3 Stir peas, cream, mustard and cheese into risotto; cook, covered, on MEDIUM (55%) 5 minutes. Stand, covered, 5 minutes. Stir in asparagus and mint.

SERVES 4

serve with a crisp green salad, followed by poached pears with cinnamon cream, page 98
per serve 19g fat; 2141kJ

chicken with soy plum sauce

PREPARATION TIME 15 MINUTES (PLUS MARINATING TIME) • COOKING TIME 55 MINUTES

1/4 cup (60ml) soy sauce
2 tablespoons dry sherry
1 tablespoon plum sauce
1 tablespoon vegetable oil
2 cloves garlic, crushed
2 teaspoons grated fresh ginger
1/4 teaspoon five-spice powder
1 tablespoon honey
1.5kg chicken
2 teaspoons cornflour
1/2 cup (125ml) water

1 Combine soy, sherry, plum sauce, oil, garlic, ginger, five-spice powder and honey in large bowl with chicken, cover; refrigerate overnight.

2 Drain chicken over medium microwave-safe bowl; reserve marinade.

3 Place chicken, breast-side down, in shallow microwave-safe dish; cook, uncovered, on MEDIUM-HIGH (70%) 20 minutes.

4 Turn chicken onto back; cook, uncovered, on MEDIUM-HIGH (70%) 10 minutes. Shield ends of drumsticks and wings with small pieces of foil to prevent overcooking (do not allow foil to touch oven walls). Cook, uncovered, on MEDIUM-HIGH (70%) a further 10 minutes or until chicken is cooked through, brushing with a little marinade twice during cooking. After cooking, check the internal temperature of the chicken with a microwave or conventional meat thermometer. The chicken must reach an internal temperature of 87°C. Stand, covered, 10 minutes.

5 Add blended cornflour and water to reserved marinade in bowl; cook, uncovered, on HIGH (100%) about 2 minutes or until sauce boils and thickens, whisking once during cooking. Serve sauce with chicken.

SERVES 4

serve with easy fried rice, page 77, and wilted Chinese greens
per serve 32.9g fat; 2090kJ

quick lamb curry with mango relish

PREPARATION TIME 25 MINUTES • COOKING TIME 15 MINUTES

- **1/4 cup (65g) Madras curry paste**
- **1 medium (150g) brown onion, sliced**
- **1 tablespoon grated fresh ginger**
- **2 cloves garlic, crushed**
- **480g lamb fillets, sliced thinly**
- **1/3 cup (80ml) yogurt**
- **2 teaspoons cornflour**
- **1/2 cup (125ml) beef stock**
- **1 tablespoon chopped fresh coriander leaves**

MANGO RELISH

- **1 medium (430g) mango, chopped coarsely**
- **1 tablespoon chopped fresh coriander leaves**
- **2 teaspoons white wine vinegar**
- **1/2 teaspoon sweet chilli sauce**

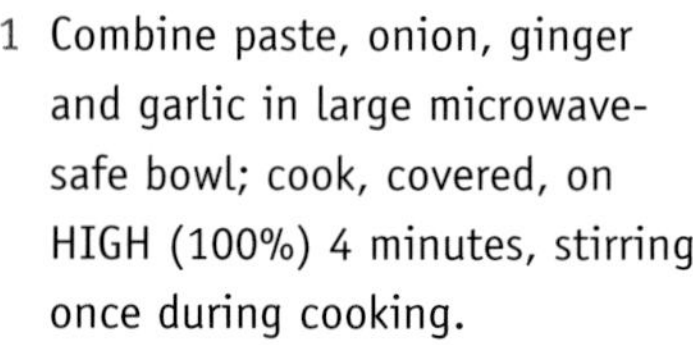

1. Combine paste, onion, ginger and garlic in large microwave-safe bowl; cook, covered, on HIGH (100%) 4 minutes, stirring once during cooking.
2. Add lamb; cook, covered, on MEDIUM-HIGH (70%) about 5 minutes or until lamb is just cooked, stirring once during cooking.
3. Stir in yogurt, blended cornflour and stock; cook, uncovered, on MEDIUM-HIGH (70%) about 5 minutes or until mixture boils and thickens slightly, stirring twice during cooking. Stir in coriander. Serve with mango relish.

Mango relish Combine all relish ingredients in medium bowl, cover; refrigerate until required.

SERVES 4

serve with steamed basmati rice, pappadams and spicy vegetable dhal, page 70

per serve 19.1g fat; 1485kJ

vegetarian nachos

PREPARATION TIME 25 MINUTES • COOKING TIME 15 MINUTES

Mexe-Beans are a canned pinto-bean mixture containing chilli, garlic, onion and various spices.

2 teaspoons olive oil
1 medium (150g) brown onion, chopped finely
2 cloves garlic, crushed
1/4 cup (60ml) tomato paste
1 teaspoon ground cumin
450g can refried beans
425g can Mexe-Beans
1 medium (250g) avocado
2 teaspoons lime juice
1 teaspoon Tabasco sauce
250g plain corn chips
1 cup (125g) coarsely grated cheddar cheese
1/2 cup (125ml) sour cream
1/2 cup (125ml) bottled salsa

1 Combine oil, onion and garlic in large microwave-safe bowl; cook, uncovered, on HIGH (100%) 4 minutes, stirring once during cooking. Add paste, cumin, refried beans and undrained Mexe-Beans; cook, uncovered, on HIGH (100%) 3 minutes.

2 Mash avocado with fork in small bowl; stir in juice and sauce. Cover tightly; refrigerate until required.

3 Divide corn chips among 4 microwave-safe plates. Spoon equal amounts of bean mixture in centre of chips, sprinkle with cheese; cook, 1 plate at a time, uncovered, on MEDIUM (55%) about 2 minutes or until cheese melts. Top Nachos with sour cream, salsa and avocado.

SERVES 4

per serve 51.3g fat; 3580kJ

ratatouille casserole

PREPARATION TIME 40 MINUTES (PLUS REFRIGERATION TIME) • COOKING TIME 50 MINUTES

The lentil polenta topping can be made the day before and kept, covered, in the refrigerator.

1 tablespoon olive oil
1 clove garlic, crushed
1 small (200g) leek, chopped
1 small (230g) eggplant, chopped coarsely
2 medium (400g) green capsicums, chopped
2 medium (400g) red capsicums, chopped
2 medium (240g) zucchini, sliced thickly
200g mushrooms, halved
1/4 cup (60ml) dry white wine
400g can tomatoes
1/2 cup (125ml) tomato puree
200g green beans, halved
2 teaspoons sugar
1 tablespoon chopped fresh oregano
2 tablespoons finely grated parmesan cheese

LENTIL POLENTA TOPPING

1/2 cup (100g) red lentils
2 cups (500ml) boiling water
1 cup (250ml) milk
1 1/2 cups (375ml) hot vegetable stock
1 1/2 cups (375ml) hot water
1 cup (170g) polenta
1/2 cup (40g) finely grated parmesan cheese
1 tablespoon finely chopped fresh parsley

Glass plates and tea towel from Empire Homewares

1 Combine oil, garlic and leek in 3-litre (12-cup) shallow microwave-safe dish; cook, uncovered, on HIGH (100%) 4 minutes, stirring once during cooking.

2 Add eggplant, capsicums, zucchini, mushrooms and wine; cook, covered, on HIGH (100%) 5 minutes.

3 Add undrained crushed tomatoes, puree, beans, sugar and oregano; cook, uncovered, on HIGH (100%) 15 minutes, stirring twice during cooking.

4 Place polenta squares on top of mixture; sprinkle with cheese. Cook, uncovered, on MEDIUM (55%) about 10 minutes.

Lentil polenta topping Combine lentils with the boiling water in large microwave-safe bowl; cook, uncovered, on HIGH (100%) 10 minutes, stirring once during cooking. Drain; cool. Combine milk, hot stock and the hot water in large microwave-safe bowl, stir in polenta; cook, uncovered, on HIGH (100%) about 8 minutes or until mixture thickens, stirring every 2 minutes. Stir in lentils, cheese and parsley. Using a damp spatula, press mixture into oiled 26cm x 32cm Swiss roll pan; cool. Cover and refrigerate until cold. Turn onto board and cut into 5cm squares.

SERVES 6

serve with a tossed Greek salad
per serve 9.7g fat; 1366kJ

satay pork noodles

PREPARATION TIME 25 MINUTES • COOKING TIME 20 MINUTES

2 tablespoons peanut oil
750g pork fillet, sliced thinly
1 medium (150g) brown onion, sliced
1 clove garlic, crushed
1/2 cup (130g) smooth peanut butter
1/4 cup (60ml) sweet chilli sauce
2/3 cup (160ml) coconut milk
3/4 cup (180ml) chicken stock
2 tablespoons lime juice
1 teaspoon sugar
1 tablespoon chopped fresh coriander leaves
450g fresh chow mein noodles
50g garlic chives, halved

1 Combine oil, pork, onion and garlic in large shallow microwave-safe dish; cook, uncovered, on MEDIUM-HIGH (70%) about 10 minutes or until pork is just cooked. Drain.

2 Add peanut butter, sauce, milk, stock, juice, sugar and coriander; cook, uncovered, on MEDIUM-HIGH (70%) about 4 minutes or until hot.

3 Rinse noodles in hot water to separate; drain. Toss chives and noodles through pork mixture in dish; cook, uncovered, on MEDIUM-HIGH (70%) about 3 minutes or until hot.

SERVES 4

serve with stir-fried bok choy
per serve 41.4g fat; 3202kJ

salmon and pasta mornay

PREPARATION TIME 25 MINUTES • COOKING TIME 30 MINUTES

200g vegeroni pasta shapes
1.5 litres (6 cups) boiling water
400g broccoli, chopped
415g can red salmon, drained
3 green onions, chopped
30g butter
1/3 cup (50g) plain flour
2 cups (500ml) milk
1/3 cup (80ml) cream
1/2 teaspoon finely grated lemon rind
2 teaspoons seeded mustard
1/2 cup (60g) coarsely grated cheddar cheese
1/2 teaspoon sweet paprika

1 Combine pasta with the boiling water in large microwave-safe bowl; cook, uncovered, on HIGH (100%) about 12 minutes or until just tender, stirring twice during cooking. Drain pasta; place in 2-litre (8-cup) shallow microwave-safe dish.

2 Cook broccoli in large microwave-safe bowl, uncovered, on HIGH (100%) 3 minutes, rinse under cold water; drain. Place broccoli, flaked salmon and onion with pasta in dish.

3 Melt butter in large microwave-safe bowl, uncovered, on HIGH (100%) 30 seconds. Whisk in flour; cook, uncovered, on HIGH (100%) 30 seconds. Whisk in milk and cream; cook, uncovered, on HIGH (100%) about 5 minutes or until sauce boils and thickens, whisking twice during cooking. Whisk in rind, mustard and cheese.

4 Pour sauce over pasta mixture, sprinkle with paprika; cook, uncovered, on MEDIUM (55%) about 10 minutes or until hot.

SERVES 4

serve with a crisp green salad
per serve 34.7g fat; 2817kJ

asian-style chilli drumsticks

PREPARATION TIME 10 MINUTES (PLUS MARINATING TIME) • COOKING TIME 25 MINUTES

8 (1.2kg) chicken drumsticks
2 tablespoons sweet chilli sauce
1/4 cup (60ml) hoisin sauce
2 tablespoons honey
3 cloves garlic, crushed
1 teaspoon grated fresh ginger
1/4 teaspoon five-spice powder
1 tablespoon white sesame seeds

1. Combine chicken in large bowl with sauces, honey, garlic, ginger and spice in large bowl, cover; refrigerate several hours.
2. Drain chicken over microwave-safe bowl; reserve marinade.
3. Place chicken, in single layer, in large shallow microwave-safe dish, with thick ends toward edge of dish; brush with 1 tablespoon marinade. Cook, uncovered, on MEDIUM-HIGH (70%) about 20 minutes or until chicken is cooked through.
4. Place sesame seeds on microwave-safe plate; cook, uncovered, on HIGH (100%) about 3 minutes or until browned lightly, stirring twice during cooking.
5. Cook remaining marinade, uncovered, on HIGH (100%) about 2 minutes or until marinade boils and thickens slightly; brush over cooked chicken. Sprinkle with seeds.

SERVES 4

serve with easy fried rice, page 77; bok choy with mushrooms, page 71
per serve 20.3 fat; 1679kJ

crustless zucchini quiche

PREPARATION TIME 20 MINUTES • COOKING TIME 35 MINUTES

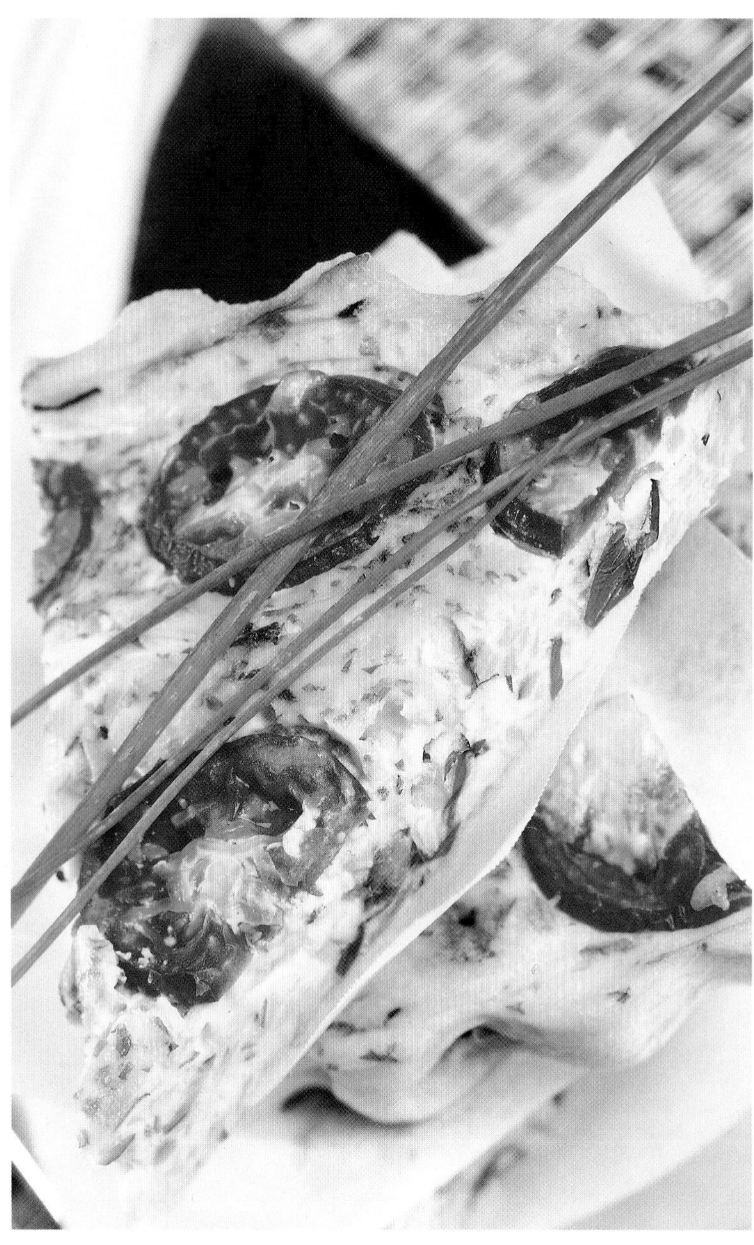

1 large (150g) zucchini, grated coarsely
1 1/2 cups (185g) coarsely grated cheddar cheese
3 green onions, chopped
1/3 cup (50g) plain flour
1 clove garlic, crushed
1 tablespoon finely chopped fresh parsley
1 cup (250ml) milk
1/2 cup (125ml) sour cream
4 eggs, beaten lightly
2 medium (150g) egg tomatoes, sliced
1/3 cup (40g) seeded black olives
1 tablespoon finely grated parmesan cheese

1 Oil shallow 24cm-round, 1.5-litre (6-cup) microwave-safe dish.

2 Combine zucchini, cheddar cheese, onion, flour, garlic, parsley, milk, cream and eggs in large bowl; mix well. Pour mixture into prepared dish, top with tomato and olives; sprinkle with parmesan cheese.

3 Cook, uncovered, on MEDIUM (55%) about 20 minutes or until centre is almost set. Stand, covered, 15 minutes.

SERVES 4

serve with a crisp green salad or coleslaw
per serve 39.4g fat; 2106kJ

cajun fish fillets with tabasco butter

PREPARATION TIME 15 MINUTES • COOKING TIME 10 MINUTES

1/4 cup (30g) sweet paprika
1/4 cup (40g) cracked black pepper
1 teaspoon cayenne pepper
2 cloves garlic, crushed
1/4 cup chopped fresh thyme
4 medium (800g) white fish fillets
60g butter
1 teaspoon Tabasco sauce

1 Combine paprika, peppers, garlic and thyme in small bowl; coat fish with pepper mixture.

2 Cook fish in large shallow microwave-safe dish, covered, on MEDIUM (55%) about 10 minutes or until cooked as desired; drain.

3 Heat butter and sauce in small microwave-safe bowl, uncovered, on HIGH (100%) about 1 minute; pour over fish.

SERVES 4

serve with cheese and chive potatoes, page 85, and corn cobs
per serve 17.9g fat; 1384kJ

chicken satay

PREPARATION TIME 30 MINUTES (PLUS MARINATING TIME) • COOKING TIME 15 MINUTES

1/2 cup (130g) crunchy peanut butter
1/4 cup (60ml) chicken stock
2 tablespoons honey
2 tablespoons soy sauce
1 tablespoon Thai red curry paste
1 tablespoon lemon juice
3 teaspoons mild curry powder
500g chicken thigh fillets, sliced
1 cup (250ml) coconut milk

1 Combine peanut butter, stock, honey, soy, paste, juice and powder in large bowl with chicken. Stir to mix well, cover; refrigerate several hours or overnight.

2 Drain chicken over medium microwave-safe bowl; reserve marinade. Thread chicken onto 8 bamboo skewers.

3 Stir milk into reserved marinade; cook, uncovered, on HIGH (100%) about 5 minutes or until sauce boils and thickens slightly, stirring once during cooking.

4 Place skewers, in single layer, in large shallow microwave-safe dish; cook, uncovered, on MEDIUM-HIGH (70%) about 8 minutes or until cooked through, turning skewers once during cooking. Serve with sauce.

SERVES 4

serve with steamed rice and stir-fried leafy green vegetables
per serve 38g fat; 2350kJ

chicken and mushroom lasagne

PREPARATION TIME 40 MINUTES • COOKING TIME 45 MINUTES

8 instant lasagne sheets
2 medium (300g) brown onions, chopped
500g field mushrooms, sliced finely
1/2 cup (125ml) dry white wine
2 cups (340g) chopped cooked chicken
2 tablespoons chopped fresh oregano
45g butter
1/3 cup (50g) plain flour
2 cups (500ml) milk
1 tablespoon seeded mustard
1 1/2 cups (185g) coarsely grated cheddar cheese

1 Place lasagne sheets in large heatproof dish, cover with boiling water; stand 5 minutes, drain, then pat dry with absorbent paper.

2 Cook onion in large microwave-safe bowl, uncovered, on HIGH (100%) 3 minutes. Add mushrooms; cook, uncovered, on HIGH (100%) 4 minutes, stirring once during cooking. Drain excess liquid away, then stir in wine, chicken and oregano.

3 Melt butter in large microwave-safe bowl, uncovered, on HIGH (100%) 30 seconds. Whisk in flour; cook, uncovered, on HIGH (100%) 30 seconds. Whisk in milk; cook, uncovered on HIGH (100%) about 5 minutes or until sauce boils and thickens, whisking twice during cooking. Whisk in mustard and half of the cheese.

4 Line base of 18cm x 28cm 2-litre (10-cup) microwave-safe dish with 2 lasagne sheets. Top with a third of the sauce, half the chicken mixture then 3 lasagne sheets. Repeat process, finishing with remaining sauce on top. Cook, uncovered, on MEDIUM (55%) 12 minutes.

5 Sprinkle with remaining cheese. Shield corners of dish with 6cm x 12cm strips of foil (do not allow foil to touch oven walls). Cook, uncovered, on MEDIUM (55%) about 10 minutes or until pasta is tender. Stand, covered, 10 minutes.

SERVES 4

serve with greek-style snow peas, page 68, and a crisp green salad
per serve 38.4g fat; 3049kJ

lamb rogan josh

PREPARATION TIME 20 MINUTES • COOKING TIME 25 MINUTES

1/3 cup (90g) rogan josh curry paste
1 large (200g) brown onion, sliced
1 clove garlic, crushed
800g lamb fillets, sliced thinly
1/4 cup (60ml) yogurt
400g can tomatoes
2 teaspoons cornflour
1 tablespoon water
1 tablespoon chopped fresh coriander leaves
1 tablespoon chopped fresh mint leaves

1 Combine paste, onion and garlic in large microwave-safe bowl; cook, covered, on HIGH (100%) 5 minutes, stirring once during cooking.

2 Stir in lamb and yogurt; cook, covered, on MEDIUM-HIGH (70%) 5 minutes, stirring once during cooking. Add undrained crushed tomatoes; cook, uncovered, on MEDIUM-HIGH (70%) 10 minutes, stirring gently once during cooking.

3 Stir in blended cornflour and water; cook, uncovered, on MEDIUM-HIGH (70%) about 2 minutes or until mixture boils and thickens slightly. Stir in herbs.

SERVES 6

serve with steamed rice and spicy vegetable dhal, page 70
per serve 16.6g fat; 1260kJ

tomato garlic prawns

PREPARATION TIME 40 MINUTES • COOKING TIME 30 MINUTES

40 (1kg) medium uncooked prawns
2 tablespoons olive oil
50g butter
1 medium (170g) red onion, chopped finely
3 cloves garlic, crushed
2 tablespoons dry red wine
3 large (750g) tomatoes, peeled, chopped
2 tablespoons tomato paste
1/2 teaspoon sugar
2 tablespoons chopped fresh parsley

1 Shell and devein prawns, leaving tails intact.

2 Combine oil, butter, onion and garlic in large microwave-safe bowl; cook, covered, on HIGH (100%) 4 minutes, stirring once during cooking.

3 Add wine, tomato, paste, sugar, and half the parsley; cook, uncovered, on HIGH (100%) about 15 minutes or until mixture thickens, stirring once during cooking.

4 Add prawns; cook, covered, on MEDIUM (55%) about 10 minutes or until prawns change in colour, stirring once during cooking. Serve sprinkled with remaining parsley.

SERVES 4

serve with steamed rice
per serve 20.8g fat; 1417kJ

macaroni cheese

PREPARATION TIME 20 MINUTES • COOKING TIME 35 MINUTES

300g macaroni
2 litres (8 cups) boiling water
2 bacon rashers, chopped finely
60g butter
½ cup (75g) plain flour
2½ cups (625ml) milk
½ cup (125ml) cream
pinch ground nutmeg
1 teaspoon Dijon mustard
1½ cups (185g) coarsely grated cheddar cheese
½ cup (40g) coarsely grated parmesan cheese
½ cup (35g) stale breadcrumbs
1 tablespoon chopped fresh chives

1 Combine pasta with the boiling water in large microwave-safe bowl; cook, uncovered, on HIGH (100%) about 12 minutes or until pasta is just tender. Drain.

2 Place bacon in large microwave-safe bowl, cover with sheet of absorbent paper; cook on HIGH (100%) 3 minutes. Discard absorbent paper; add butter, stir until melted.

3 Whisk in flour; cook, uncovered, on HIGH (100%) 1 minute. Whisk in milk and cream; cook, uncovered, on HIGH (100%) about 6 minutes or until sauce boils and thickens, whisking twice during cooking.

4 Add nutmeg, mustard and half the combined cheeses, stir until cheeses melt; add pasta, mix well.

5 Spoon pasta mixture into oiled 2-litre (8-cup) shallow microwave-safe dish. Top with breadcrumbs, remaining cheeses and chives; cook, uncovered, on MEDIUM (55%) about 15 minutes or until hot.

SERVES 4

serve with a tossed salad
per serve 55.5g fat; 4014kJ

honey mustard chicken with fruity couscous

PREPARATION TIME 25 MINUTES • COOKING TIME 25 MINUTES

1/2 cup (125ml) honey
1 tablespoon seeded mustard
2 tablespoons lemon juice
2 teaspoons finely chopped fresh rosemary
6 (660g) chicken thigh fillets, halved
2 teaspoons cornflour
2 teaspoons water
200ml yogurt
1/2 teaspoon garam masala
1 tablespoon shredded fresh mint leaves

FRUITY COUSCOUS
20g butter
1 medium (150g) brown onion, sliced thinly
1 teaspoon garam masala
1/4 cup (35g) dried currants
1/4 cup (35g) finely chopped dried apricots
1 1/4 cups (310ml) hot chicken stock
1 cup (200g) couscous

1 Combine honey, mustard, juice and rosemary in large shallow microwave-safe dish; cook, uncovered, on HIGH (100%) 2 minutes.

2 Add chicken, in single layer, to dish, cook, uncovered, on MEDIUM-HIGH (70%) about 10 minutes or until chicken is cooked through, rearranging once during cooking. Remove chicken; cover to keep warm.

3 Stir blended cornflour and water into juices in dish; cook, uncovered, on HIGH (100%) about 2 minutes or until sauce boils and thickens. Return chicken to dish; coat with sauce.

4 Combine yogurt, garam masala and mint in small bowl; serve with chicken and fruity couscous.

Fruity couscous Combine butter, onion and garam masala in large microwave-safe bowl; cook, uncovered, on HIGH (100%) 4 minutes, stirring once during cooking. Add currants, apricots and stock; cook, covered, on HIGH (100%) about 2 minutes or until boiling. Stir in couscous; stand, covered, 5 minutes. Fluff with fork.

SERVES 4

serve with warm capsicum salad, page 73
per serve 13.8g fat; 2532kJ

accompaniments

An accompaniment can lift an ordinary main course into the realm of the very special, one that family and friends will ask for again and again. Here, we bring you combinations of vegetable recipes which draw on cuisines from around the world, plus old favourites with delicious sauces – all super-quick to cook so they are just as good for family meals as they are for elegant entertaining.

sweet chilli, kumara and bean toss

PREPARATION TIME 10 MINUTES
COOKING TIME 10 MINUTES

1 medium (400g) kumara
300g green beans
2 tablespoons water
1 tablespoon honey
1 tablespoon sweet chilli sauce
1 teaspoon grated fresh ginger
60g butter

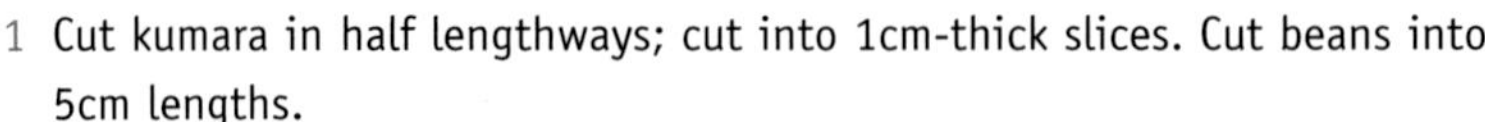

1. Cut kumara in half lengthways; cut into 1cm-thick slices. Cut beans into 5cm lengths.
2. Cook kumara and the water in large microwave-safe bowl, covered, on HIGH (100%) 3 minutes. Add beans; cook, covered, on HIGH (100%) 5 minutes. Drain; cover vegetables to keep warm.
3. Combine remaining ingredients in small microwave-safe bowl; cook, uncovered, on HIGH (100%) about 1 minute or until butter has melted.
4. Gently toss butter mixture through hot kumara and beans.

SERVES 4

per serve 12.7g fat; 858kJ

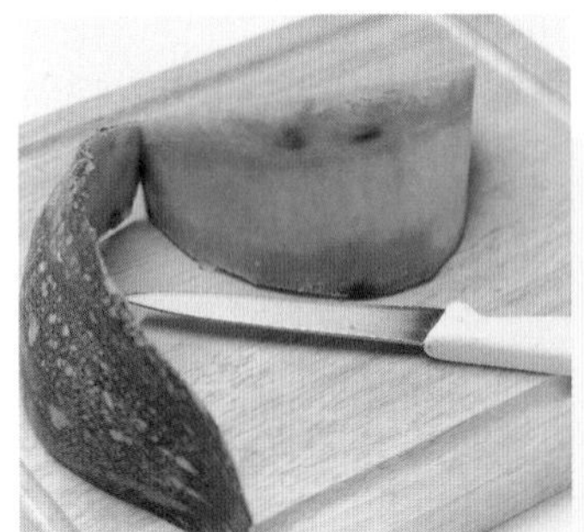

peeling pumpkin

This is an invaluable tip for any cook who has ever wrestled with a tough pumpkin, attempting to cut and peel it to use in soup or as a vegetable. Struggle no more! Just place a 500g piece of pumpkin on the turntable; cook, uncovered, on HIGH (100%) for 2 minutes. You won't believe how easy it is to chop.

greek-style snow peas

PREPARATION TIME 20 MINUTES • COOKING TIME 10 MINUTES

200g snow peas, trimmed
30g butter
1 medium (150g) brown onion, sliced thinly
1 clove garlic, crushed
3 small (400g) tomatoes, chopped
1 teaspoon chopped fresh thyme
$^1/_2$ cup (60g) black olives, seeded
150g fetta cheese, crumbled

1 Rinse snow peas under cold water; cook in shallow microwave-safe dish, covered, on HIGH (100%) 1 minute. Drain.

2 Combine butter, onion and garlic in same dish; cook, uncovered, on HIGH (100%) 4 minutes, stirring once during cooking.

3 Stir in tomato and thyme; cook, covered, on HIGH (100%) 2 minutes.

4 Stir in snow peas, olives and cheese.

SERVES 6

per serve 12.2g fat; 606kJ

cheese and basil-seasoned zucchini

PREPARATION TIME 15 MINUTES • COOKING TIME 15 MINUTES

6 medium (720g) zucchini, halved lengthways
3 bacon rashers, chopped finely
1 1/2 tablespoons chopped fresh basil leaves
3/4 cup (60g) finely grated parmesan cheese
1/2 cup (35g) stale breadcrumbs

1 Place zucchini on large microwave-safe plate with thick ends toward edge of plate. Cover, cook on HIGH (100%) about 6 minutes or until tender.

2 Scoop out flesh from zucchini, leaving 1cm-thick shell. Chop zucchini flesh; combine with remaining ingredients in small bowl.

3 Spoon filling mixture into zucchini shells, cover; cook on MEDIUM (55%) about 6 minutes or until just heated through.

SERVES 6

per serve 7.3g fat; 502kJ

spicy vegetable dhal

PREPARATION TIME 30 MINUTES • COOKING TIME 30 MINUTES

Red lentils are called masoor dhal in Indian kitchens.

1 cup (200g) red lentils
1 teaspoon chopped fresh ginger
1 clove garlic, quartered
1 small fresh red chilli, seeded, chopped coarsely
1 trimmed (75g) stick celery, chopped finely
3 green onions, chopped coarsely
1 medium (120g) carrot, chopped coarsely
2 tablespoons chopped fresh coriander leaves
1 tablespoon lemon juice
3 cups (750ml) hot water
1 teaspoon garam masala
1/4 teaspoon ground turmeric
1 teaspoon ground coriander
1 teaspoon cumin seeds

1 Rinse and drain lentils. Combine lentils, ginger, garlic, chilli, celery, onion, carrot, fresh coriander, juice and the water in large microwave-safe bowl; cook, covered, on HIGH (100%) about 20 minutes or until lentils and vegetables are soft, stirring once during cooking. Cool.

2 Blend or process mixture, in batches, until smooth; return to same bowl.

3 Cook ground spices and seeds in small microwave-safe bowl, uncovered, on HIGH (100%) 1 minute; stir into lentil mixture. Cook, uncovered, on HIGH (100%) about 5 minutes or until dhal thickens, stirring once during cooking.

SERVES 6

per serve 0.7g fat; 406kJ

bok choy with mushrooms

PREPARATION TIME 10 MINUTES • COOKING TIME 5 MINUTES

400g bok choy
150g oyster mushrooms
1/2 teaspoon sesame oil
1 tablespoon salt-reduced soy sauce
1 tablespoon oyster sauce
1 tablespoon sesame seeds

1 Rinse bok choy well under cold water. Coarsely shred leaves; cut trimmed stems in half lengthways.

2 Place stems around edge of large shallow microwave-safe dish; place leaves in centre of dish. Cook, covered, on HIGH (100%) 2 minutes.

3 Combine mushrooms, oil, sauces and seeds in large microwave-safe bowl; cook, covered, on HIGH (100%) about 3 minutes or until mushrooms are tender, stirring once during cooking.

4 Combine drained bok choy and mushrooms in serving dish and mix well.

SERVES 4

per serve 2.3g fat; 201kJ

baba ghanoush

PREPARATION TIME 15 MINUTES • COOKING TIME 30 MINUTES

2 large (1kg) eggplants
1/4 cup (60ml) olive oil
2 tablespoons lemon juice
1 clove garlic, quartered
1/4 cup (60ml) tahini
2 teaspoons ground cumin
2/3 cup fresh flat-leaf parsley sprigs

1 Prick eggplants all over with fork; place on microwave turntable. Cook, uncovered, on HIGH (100%) about 15 minutes or until soft, rotating eggplants halfway through cooking. Stand eggplants 15 minutes.

2 Peel eggplants, chop flesh roughly.

3 Blend or process eggplant flesh with remaining ingredients until pureed.

SERVES 4

per serve 24.3g fat; 1132kJ

warm capsicum salad

PREPARATION TIME 15 MINUTES • COOKING TIME 15 MINUTES

2 tablespoons pine nuts
1 small (80g) brown onion, sliced
1 medium (200g) red capsicum, sliced thickly
1 medium (200g) yellow capsicum, sliced thickly
1 medium (200g) green capsicum, sliced thickly
2 tablespoons extra virgin olive oil
1 clove garlic, crushed
2 teaspoons balsamic vinegar

1 Cook nuts in small microwave-safe bowl, uncovered, on HIGH (100%) about 3 minutes or until browned lightly, stirring twice during cooking.

2 Combine onion, capsicums, oil and garlic in large microwave-safe bowl; cook, covered, on HIGH (100%) about 8 minutes or until capsicum is tender, stirring once during cooking. Stand 2 minutes before stirring in vinegar and nuts.

SERVES 4

per serve 14.4g fat; 668kJ

caponata

PREPARATION TIME 25 MINUTES (PLUS STANDING TIME) • COOKING TIME 35 MINUTES

2 small (460g) eggplants
coarse cooking salt
1/4 cup (60ml) olive oil
4 medium (600g) brown onions, chopped
2 cloves garlic, crushed
2 trimmed (150g) sticks celery, chopped
1 cup (120g) seeded green olives, halved
2 x 400g cans tomatoes
1 teaspoon cracked black pepper
1 tablespoon sugar
1/2 cup (125ml) red wine vinegar
2 tablespoons drained capers
2 tablespoons chopped fresh parsley
2 tablespoons chopped fresh basil leaves

1. Chop eggplants into 2cm cubes, place in colander, sprinkle with salt; stand 30 minutes. Rinse eggplant under cold water; drain on absorbent paper.
2. Combine oil and eggplant in large microwave-safe bowl; cook, uncovered, on HIGH (100%) about 10 minutes or until tender, stirring once during cooking. Remove eggplant from bowl.
3. Place onion, garlic and celery in same bowl; cook, covered, on HIGH (100%) about 10 minutes or until onion is very soft, stirring once during cooking.
4. Add olives, undrained crushed tomatoes and pepper; cook, uncovered, on HIGH (100%) 10 minutes, stirring once during cooking.
5. Stir in sugar, vinegar and capers; cook, uncovered, on HIGH (100%) 5 minutes. Stir in eggplant and herbs, cool.

SERVES 6

per serve 10.9g fat; 756kJ

cauliflower au gratin

PREPARATION TIME 20 MINUTES • COOKING TIME 15 MINUTES

1 small (1kg) cauliflower
30g butter
1 tablespoon plain flour
2 green onions, chopped
3/4 cup (180ml) milk
3/4 cup (90g) coarsely grated cheddar cheese
1/3 cup (35g) Corn Flake Crumbs
15g butter, extra
1 tablespoon finely chopped fresh parsley

1. Trim cauliflower, cut into florets. Rinse florets under cold water; arrange in large shallow microwave-safe dish, stem ends towards edge of dish. Cook, covered, on HIGH (100%) 5 minutes; drain.
2. Melt butter in microwave-safe jug, uncovered, on HIGH (100%) 30 seconds. Whisk in flour and onion, then gradually whisk in milk; cook, uncovered, on HIGH (100%) about 2 minutes or until sauce boils and thickens, whisking once during cooking. Stir in cheese.
3. Combine Crumbs, extra butter and parsley in small microwave-safe bowl; cook, uncovered, on HIGH (100%) 1 minute.
4. Pour sauce over cauliflower in dish; cook, uncovered, on MEDIUM (55%) about 4 minutes or until hot. Serve sprinkled with crumb mixture.

SERVES 6

serve with mustard lamb racks with sundried tomatoes, page 33
per serve 12.6g fat; 709kJ

corn cobs with herb and bacon butter

PREPARATION TIME 15 MINUTES • COOKING TIME 15 MINUTES

4 (1kg) corn cobs, trimmed
1 bacon rasher, chopped
1 green onion, chopped
1/2 teaspoon sambal oelek
60g butter, melted
2 teaspoons chopped fresh parsley
1 teaspoon chopped fresh basil leaves
1 teaspoon chopped fresh thyme

1 Rinse corn under cold water; wrap each cob in microwave-safe plastic wrap.

2 Place corn around edge of microwave turntable; cook on HIGH (100%) 10 minutes, turning corn once during cooking. Cut corn into 4cm pieces; cover to keep warm.

3 Combine bacon, onion and sambal in small microwave-safe bowl; cook, covered, on HIGH (100%) 2 minutes, stirring once during cooking. Drain bacon mixture on absorbent paper.

4 Melt butter in same small bowl on HIGH (100%) 30 seconds; add bacon mixture and herbs. Serve corn with bacon butter.

SERVES 4

per serve 16.3g fat; 1260kJ

easy fried rice

PREPARATION TIME 15 MINUTES • COOKING TIME 20 MINUTES

1 cup (200g) white long-grain rice
6cm strip lemon rind
3 cups (750ml) boiling water
2 teaspoons vegetable oil
2 bacon rashers, chopped finely
1 medium (120g) carrot, sliced thinly
1 trimmed (75g) stick celery, sliced thinly
1 clove garlic, crushed
1 teaspoon grated fresh ginger
80g button mushrooms, sliced
2 green onions, sliced
1 tablespoon soy sauce

1 Cook rice, rind and the water in large microwave-safe bowl, uncovered, on HIGH (100%) about 12 minutes or until rice is tender, stirring once during cooking. Rinse rice well; drain, discard rind.

2 Combine oil, bacon, carrot, celery, garlic and ginger in large microwave-safe bowl; cook, covered, on HIGH (100%) about 5 minutes or until vegetables are just tender, stirring once during cooking. Drain away excess liquid.

3 Add rice, mushrooms, onion and sauce to bowl; mix to combine. Cook, covered, on HIGH (100%) about 4 minutes or until hot.

SERVES 4

per serve 6.3g fat; 1087kJ

broccoli with pine nuts

PREPARATION TIME 20 MINUTES • COOKING TIME 15 MINUTES

800g broccoli
2 tablespoons pine nuts
3 bacon rashers, chopped finely
1/4 cup (30g) coarsely grated cheddar cheese
1/4 cup (20g) coarsely grated parmesan cheese

1 Cut broccoli into florets; rinse under cold water. Arrange florets in shallow microwave-safe dish, stem ends towards edge of dish. Cook, covered, on HIGH (100%) about 3 minutes or until just tender; drain.

2 Cook nuts on microwave-safe plate, uncovered, on HIGH (100%) about 3 minutes or until browned lightly, stirring twice during cooking.

3 Cook bacon between double thicknesses of absorbent paper, on HIGH (100%) about 3 minutes or until bacon is crisp.

4 Sprinkle nuts, bacon and cheeses over broccoli in dish; cook, uncovered, on MEDIUM (55%) about 2 minutes or until cheeses are melted.

SERVES 6

per serve 10.6g fat; 627kJ

bacon and cheese potatoes

PREPARATION TIME 15 MINUTES • COOKING TIME 15 MINUTES

16 (640g) tiny new potatoes
2 tablespoons water
1/4 cup (20g) finely grated parmesan cheese
2 bacon rashers, chopped finely
1/4 cup (60ml) cream
1 clove garlic, crushed
1 tablespoon chopped fresh parsley

1 Prick potatoes all over with fork. Cook potatoes, in single layer, with the water in shallow microwave-safe dish, covered, on HIGH (100%) about 10 minutes or until tender, rearranging potatoes once during cooking; drain.

2 Sprinkle potatoes with cheese and bacon in dish; pour over combined cream and garlic. Cook, uncovered, on MEDIUM (55%) 5 minutes. Sprinkle potatoes with parsley.

SERVES 4

per serve 11.8g fat; 956kJ

curried vegetable and rice medley

PREPARATION TIME 25 MINUTES • COOKING TIME 15 MINUTES

You will need to cook 2/3 cup (130g) white long-grain rice for this recipe.

1 small (150g) red capsicum
2 medium (240g) carrots
2 teaspoons vegetable oil
1 medium (150g) brown onion, chopped finely
1 clove garlic, crushed
1 teaspoon mild curry powder
1 teaspoon ground cumin
2 tablespoons fruit chutney
250g broccoli, chopped
125g button mushrooms, sliced thinly
1/2 cup (125ml) vegetable stock
2 cups cooked white rice

1. Cut capsicum and carrots into thin strips.
2. Combine oil, onion, garlic and spices in large microwave-safe bowl; cook, uncovered, on HIGH (100%) 4 minutes, stirring once during cooking.
3. Add chutney and vegetables; cook, covered, on HIGH (100%) 5 minutes.
4. Add stock and rice; cook, covered, on HIGH (100%) about 4 minutes or until hot, stirring once during cooking.

SERVES 6

per serve 2.1g fat; 421kJ

potato and bacon casserole

PREPARATION TIME 15 MINUTES • COOKING TIME 30 MINUTES

4 bacon rashers, chopped
750g tiny new potatoes, sliced thinly
1 medium (150g) brown onion, sliced thinly
1/2 x 40g packet salt-reduced chicken noodle soup mix
1 cup (250ml) cream
1 cup (125g) coarsely grated cheddar cheese

1. Cook bacon between double thicknesses of absorbent paper, on HIGH (100%) about 5 minutes or until crisp.
2. Place potato slices in 1.5-litre (6-cup) shallow microwave-safe dish; cook, covered, on HIGH (100%) 5 minutes.
3. Sprinkle onion, bacon and dry soup mix over potato in dish; pour over cream. Cook, covered, on MEDIUM (55%) about 15 minutes or until potato is tender.
4. Sprinkle potato with cheese; cook, uncovered, on MEDIUM (55%) about 2 minutes or until cheese melts.

SERVES 6

per serve 30g fat; 1700kJ

asparagus with hollandaise sauce

PREPARATION TIME 15 MINUTES • COOKING TIME 5 MINUTES

500g fresh asparagus
1 tablespoon water
125g butter
2 egg yolks
1½ tablespoons water, extra
1 tablespoon lemon juice
pinch cayenne pepper

1 Snap tough ends from asparagus. Arrange asparagus, thick ends towards edge of dish, in no more than 2 layers, in large microwave-safe dish, sprinkle with the water. Cook, covered, on HIGH (100%) 3 minutes; drain. Cover to keep warm.

2 Melt butter in microwave-safe jug, uncovered, on HIGH (100%) 1 minute.

3 Whisk egg yolks, the extra water and juice in small microwave-safe bowl; cook, uncovered, on MEDIUM (55%) 1 minute, whisking every 15 seconds, or until sauce thickens. Do not allow to boil.

4 Remove sauce from microwave oven. Whisking constantly, add melted butter, a few drops at a time, until mixture starts to thicken. Continue to add butter, in a thin stream, whisking constantly, until all butter is used; whisk in pepper. Serve hollandaise sauce over hot asparagus.

SERVES 4

per serve 28.5g fat; 1150kJ

layered eggplant and tomato

PREPARATION TIME 25 MINUTES (PLUS STANDING TIME) • **COOKING TIME** 15 MINUTES

2 medium (600g) eggplants
coarse cooking salt
3 large (750g) tomatoes, peeled, sliced thickly
1 tablespoon chopped fresh basil leaves
1 tablespoon chopped fresh oregano
$^1/_2$ teaspoon seasoned pepper
1 cup (100g) coarsely grated mozzarella cheese

1 Cut eggplants into 1cm-thick slices. Place slices in colander, sprinkle with salt; stand 30 minutes. Rinse slices under cold water; drain, pat dry with absorbent paper.

2 Overlap eggplant slices in 1.5-litre (6-cup) shallow microwave-safe dish; cook, covered, on HIGH (100%) about 5 minutes or until tender, turning eggplant once during cooking. Drain on absorbent paper.

3 Place half of the eggplant over base of same dish, overlapping slices if necessary. Top with half of the tomato and half of the combined herbs, pepper and cheese. Repeat layers with remaining eggplant, tomato and herb mixture.

4 Cook, uncovered, on MEDIUM (55%) about 10 minutes or until cheese melts and vegetables are hot.

SERVES 6

per serve 4g fat; 353kJ

spinach rice

PREPARATION TIME 20 MINUTES • COOKING TIME 25 MINUTES

30g butter
1 tablespoon olive oil
2 medium (300g) brown onions, chopped finely
2 cloves garlic, crushed
2 cups (400g) white long-grain rice
1 litre (4 cups) boiling chicken stock
50g spinach, chopped
2 small (260g) tomatoes, seeded, chopped
1/4 cup (20g) finely grated parmesan cheese

1. Combine butter, oil, onion and garlic in large microwave-safe bowl; cook, uncovered, on HIGH (100%) 5 minutes, stirring once during cooking.
2. Add rice; cook, uncovered, on HIGH (100%) 1 minute.
3. Add stock; cook, covered, on HIGH (100%) 12 minutes, stirring once during cooking. Stand, covered, 5 minutes.
4. Add spinach, tomato and cheese; stir until spinach just wilts.

SERVES 6

per serve fat 9.2g; 1556kJ

cheese and chive potatoes

PREPARATION TIME 25 MINUTES • COOKING TIME 25 MINUTES

4 medium (800g) potatoes
1 cup (125g) coarsely grated cheddar cheese
1 clove garlic, crushed
1 small (100g) red onion, chopped finely
1 tablespoon finely chopped fresh chives

1 Prick skin of potatoes in several places; place on absorbent paper around edge of microwave oven turntable. Cook potatoes, uncovered, on HIGH (100%) about 12 minutes or until tender. Stand 5 minutes before cutting off a third from top of each potato.

2 Scoop out flesh from potatoes and tops, leaving 1cm-thick shells; discard skins from tops.

3 Combine mashed potato flesh in medium bowl with cheese, garlic and onion; mix well.

4 Spoon potato mixture into potato shells, place on absorbent paper around edge of microwave turntable; cook, uncovered, on MEDIUM (55%) about 5 minutes or until hot. Sprinkle with chives.

SERVES 4

per serve fat 10.8g; 1103kJ

desserts

Traditional favourites for dessert (try the lemon delicious), scrumptious nibbles to have with coffee, luscious cakes and inviting fruit puddings – everything to tempt those with a sweet tooth – can be made quickly and easily in your microwave oven.

poached peaches with custard

PREPARATION TIME 20 MINUTES (PLUS REFRIGERATION)
COOKING TIME 20 MINUTES

3 cups (750ml) water
1 cup (250ml) orange juice
$1\frac{1}{2}$ cups (330g) caster sugar
4 medium (800g) firm peaches
1 teaspoon cornflour
2 teaspoons water, extra

CUSTARD

1 cup (250ml) milk
3 egg yolks
$\frac{1}{3}$ cup (75g) caster sugar

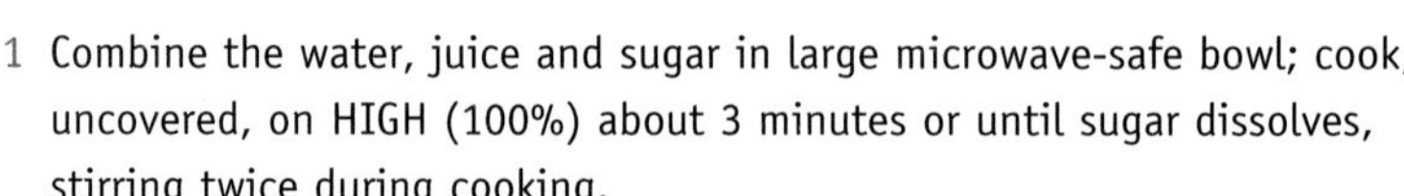

1 Combine the water, juice and sugar in large microwave-safe bowl; cook, uncovered, on HIGH (100%) about 3 minutes or until sugar dissolves, stirring twice during cooking.
2 Add peaches; cook, covered, on HIGH (100%) about 6 minutes or until tender. Cover peaches; refrigerate 3 hours.
3 Remove peaches from syrup; peel, reserve syrup.
4 Strain 1 cup (250ml) syrup into microwave-safe jug; stir in blended cornflour and extra water. Cook, uncovered, on HIGH (100%) about 3 minutes or until syrup boils and thickens slightly, whisking twice during cooking; cool.
5 Serve peaches with syrup and custard.

Custard Heat milk in microwave-safe jug on MEDIUM-HIGH (70%) 1 minute. Whisk in combined yolks and sugar; cook, uncovered, on MEDIUM (55%) about 5 minutes or until custard thickens slightly, whisking twice during cooking. Cover surface closely with plastic wrap; refrigerate until required.

SERVES 4

per serve 6.8g fat; 2297kJ

how to melt chocolate

Place 100g chopped chocolate in a small microwave-safe bowl; cook, uncovered, on MEDIUM (55%) about 2 minutes. Chocolate will hold its shape after heating; stir before cooking further.

lemon and blueberry self-saucing pudding

PREPARATION TIME 15 MINUTES • COOKING TIME 20 MINUTES

60g butter

1½ cups (225g) self-raising flour

1 cup (220g) caster sugar

1 tablespoon grated lemon rind

¾ cup (180ml) milk

1 cup (150g) fresh blueberries

1 cup (200g) firmly packed brown sugar

½ cup (125ml) lemon juice

1½ cups (375ml) boiling water

1 Melt butter in a deep 3-litre (12-cup) microwave-safe dish, uncovered, on HIGH (100%) 1 minute. Add flour, caster sugar, rind and milk; whisk until smooth, stir in blueberries.

2 Sprinkle brown sugar evenly over top; carefully pour combined juice and boiling water over brown sugar.

3 Cook, uncovered, on HIGH (100%) about 12 minutes or until just cooked in centre; stand 5 minutes before serving.

SERVES 6

per serve 9.9g fat; 2099kJ

strawberry-glazed cheesecakes

PREPARATION TIME 30 MINUTES (PLUS REFRIGERATION TIME) • **COOKING TIME** 10 MINUTES

1½ cups (150g) plain sweet biscuit crumbs
80g butter, melted
¼ cup (60ml) strawberry jam, warmed
250g strawberries, halved

FILLING

250g packet cream cheese
⅓ cup (75g) caster sugar
2 tablespoons cornflour
300ml sour cream
3 eggs, beaten lightly
2 teaspoons finely grated lemon rind
2 teaspoons lemon juice

1 Grease four 1¼-cup (310ml) microwave-safe dishes, line bases of each dish with baking paper.

2 Combine crumbs and butter in small bowl; divide among prepared dishes, press over bases. Pour filling into prepared dishes; refrigerate about 3 hours or until set.

3 Just before serving, run a knife around edge of dishes. Turn out cheesecakes; brush tops with sieved jam, decorate with strawberries, brush with remaining jam.

Filling Beat softened cream cheese, sugar and cornflour in small bowl with electric mixer until combined. Add remaining ingredients; beat until smooth. Transfer mixture to large microwave-safe bowl; cook, uncovered, on MEDIUM (55%) about 10 minutes or until mixture is extremely thick, whisking after each minute.

SERVES 4

per serve 77.7g fat; 4239kJ

apple and pecan cake

PREPARATION TIME 20 MINUTES • COOKING TIME 15 MINUTES

1/3 cup (35g) hazelnut meal
90g butter, softened
1 1/2 cups (225g) self-raising flour
1 teaspoon ground cinnamon
3/4 cup (150g) firmly packed brown sugar
1/4 cup (60ml) maple-flavoured syrup
3 eggs
1 cup (125g) chopped pecans
1/2 cup (85g) chopped raisins
1 large (200g) apple, peeled, grated

1 Grease 21cm microwave-safe ring pan, sprinkle base and sides with hazelnut meal.

2 Beat butter, flour, cinnamon, sugar, syrup and eggs in medium bowl with electric mixer, on low speed, until ingredients are combined. Then beat on medium speed about 2 minutes or until mixture is smooth and changed in colour.

3 Stir in nuts, raisins and apple. Spread mixture into prepared dish; cook, uncovered, on MEDIUM-HIGH (70%) about 10 minutes or until just cooked. Stand 5 minutes before turning onto wire rack to cool.

SERVES 8

per serve 26g fat; 2005kJ

peanut cookies

PREPARATION TIME 20 MINUTES • COOKING TIME 8 MINUTES

1/2 cup (130g) smooth peanut butter
90g soft butter
3/4 cup (165g) raw sugar
1 egg
1 teaspoon vanilla essence
11/2 cups (225g) plain flour
1/2 cup (75g) unsalted roasted peanuts
14 red glacé cherries, halved

1. Beat peanut butter, butter, sugar, egg, essence and flour in small bowl with electric mixer until combined; stir in peanuts.
2. Roll level tablespoons of mixture into balls. Cover microwave turntable with baking paper, place 7 balls evenly around turntable about 2cm from edge.
3. Flatten balls slightly, top with cherry halves. Cook, uncovered, on HIGH (100%) 2 minutes.
4. Slide paper and cookies onto wire rack; stand 5 minutes before lifting from paper onto rack to cool. Repeat with remaining mixture and cherries.

MAKES 28

per serve 6.6g fat; 527kJ

zucchini walnut loaf

PREPARATION TIME 20 MINUTES • COOKING TIME 20 MINUTES

You will need about 2 small (180g) zucchini for this recipe.

1/3 cup (40g) walnut pieces
2 eggs
3/4 cup (150g) firmly packed brown sugar
3/4 cup (180ml) vegetable oil
1 teaspoon mixed spice
1 cup coarsely grated zucchini
2/3 cup (80g) walnut pieces, extra
3/4 cup (110g) plain flour
1 cup (150g) self-raising flour

1 Grease 12cm x 22cm microwave-safe loaf pan; line base with baking paper. Crush nuts finely, press half onto sides of pan.

2 Whisk eggs, sugar, oil and spice in large bowl until smooth; add, in 2 batches, zucchini, extra nuts and flours. Spread mixture into prepared pan; sprinkle with remaining crushed nuts.

3 Cook, uncovered, on MEDIUM-HIGH (70%) about 9 minutes or until centre is just cooked.

4 Cover with greased foil; stand 10 minutes before turning onto wire rack to cool.

SERVES 8

per serve 33.9g fat; 2074kJ

pumpkin pecan muffins

PREPARATION TIME 20 MINUTES • COOKING TIME 10 MINUTES

You will need to cook about 300g pumpkin for this recipe.

$1\frac{1}{2}$ cups (225g) self-raising flour
$\frac{1}{2}$ teaspoon ground cinnamon
$\frac{1}{2}$ teaspoon mixed spice
$\frac{1}{3}$ cup (75g) firmly packed brown sugar
$\frac{1}{3}$ cup (80ml) vegetable oil
2 eggs, beaten lightly
$\frac{3}{4}$ cup cooked mashed pumpkin
$\frac{1}{2}$ cup (60g) chopped pecans
$\frac{1}{4}$ cup (60ml) cream
$\frac{1}{4}$ cup (30g) chopped pecans, extra

1 Grease two 6-hole ($\frac{1}{3}$ cup/80ml) microwave-safe muffin pans.

2 Combine flour, spices, sugar, oil, egg, pumpkin, nuts and cream in large bowl, stir until just combined. Spoon mixture into prepared pans; sprinkle with extra nuts.

3 Cook 1 pan at a time, uncovered, on MEDIUM-HIGH (70%) about 4 minutes or until muffins are just cooked in the centre. Stand 1 minute before turning muffins onto wire rack.

MAKES 12

per serve 15.3g fat; 1000kJ

mocha self-saucing pudding

PREPARATION TIME 15 MINUTES • **COOKING TIME** 20 MINUTES

60g butter
1 cup (220g) caster sugar
$1\frac{1}{2}$ cups (225g) self-raising flour
$\frac{3}{4}$ cup (180ml) milk
$\frac{1}{2}$ cup (50g) cocoa
1 cup (200g) firmly packed brown sugar
2 teaspoons instant coffee powder
2 cups (500ml) boiling water

1 Melt butter in deep 3-litre (12-cup) microwave-safe dish, uncovered, on HIGH (100%) 1 minute. Stir in caster sugar, flour, milk and half the cocoa; whisk until smooth.

2 Sift combined remaining cocoa, brown sugar and coffee powder evenly over top; carefully pour the boiling water over brown sugar mixture.

3 Cook, uncovered, on HIGH (100%) about 12 minutes or until just cooked in centre; stand 5 minutes before serving.

SERVES 6

per serve 11g fat; 2128kJ

chocolate caramel slice

PREPARATION TIME 20 MINUTES (PLUS REFRIGERATION TIME) • COOKING TIME 15 MINUTES

1/2 cup (45g) desiccated coconut
160g butter, melted
2 cups (200g) plain chocolate biscuit crumbs
400g can sweetened condensed milk
60g butter, extra
2 tablespoons maple-flavoured syrup
100g dark chocolate, chopped
2 teaspoons vegetable oil

1. Grease shallow 18cm x 28cm microwave-safe dish, line base and sides with baking paper.
2. Cook coconut in medium microwave-safe bowl, uncovered, on HIGH (100%) about 3 minutes or until browned lightly, stirring 3 times during cooking; remove from bowl, cool.
3. Melt butter in same bowl, uncovered, on HIGH (100%) 1 minute. Add coconut and crumbs, stir well. Press over base of prepared dish, refrigerate until firm.
4. Combine milk, extra butter and syrup in large glass microwave-safe bowl; cook, uncovered, on HIGH (100%) about 8 minutes or until thick and golden brown, whisking every minute. Spread quickly over biscuit base; refrigerate until firm.
5. Melt chocolate with oil in small microwave-safe bowl, uncovered, on MEDIUM (55%) 1 1/2 minutes, stirring twice during cooking. Spread over caramel mixture. Mark chocolate with fork; refrigerate slice until firm.

MAKES 27 PIECES

per serve 11.9g fat; 748kJ

karen's sticky toffee pudding

PREPARATION TIME 25 MINUTES • COOKING TIME 25 MINUTES

This mixture will also make 18 sticky toffee pudding muffins. Pour mixture into lightly greased 2/3-cup capacity holes of microwave-safe muffin pans. Cook, uncovered, on MEDIUM-HIGH (70%) about 3½ minutes or until muffins are almost cooked through.

1 cup (170g) seeded dates, chopped
1¼ cups (310ml) hot water
1 teaspoon bicarbonate of soda
80g butter, chopped
¾ cup (165g) raw sugar
2 eggs
1¼ cups (185g) self-raising flour

CARAMEL SAUCE

¾ cup (150g) firmly packed brown sugar
2/3 cup (160ml) cream
30g butter, chopped

1. Lightly grease 21cm microwave-safe ring pan, line base with baking paper.
2. Combine dates and water in medium microwave-safe bowl; cook, uncovered on HIGH (100%) 4 minutes, stirring once during cooking.
3. Stir in soda (mixture will foam); cool 5 minutes.
4. Blend or process date mixture with remaining ingredients until combined; spread into prepared pan.
5. Cook, uncovered, on MEDIUM-HIGH (70%) 8 minutes. Stand 5 minutes before turning onto wire rack to cool. Serve warm with caramel sauce.

Caramel sauce Combine all ingredients in medium microwave-safe bowl. Cook, uncovered, on HIGH (100%) about 7 minutes or until caramel has thickened, whisking after each minute.

SERVES 8

per serve 21.8g fat; 2031kJ

poached pears with cinnamon cream

PREPARATION TIME 20 MINUTES (PLUS REFRIGERATION TIME) • **COOKING TIME** 20 MINUTES

4 small (720g) firm pears
1 cup (250ml) dry red wine
1 cup (250ml) water
1/2 cup (110g) caster sugar
1 cinnamon stick
1 tablespoon caster sugar, extra
1 teaspoon cornflour
2 teaspoons water, extra

CINNAMON CREAM

300ml thickened cream
1 tablespoon caster sugar
1 teaspoon ground cinnamon

1 Level bases of pears to sit flat; peel. Combine wine, the water, sugar and cinnamon stick in large microwave-safe dish; cook, uncovered, on HIGH (100%) 3 minutes. Stir until sugar dissolves.

2 Place pears upright in poaching syrup; cook, covered, on HIGH (100%) 5 minutes. Rotate pears 180 degrees; cook, covered, on HIGH (100%) about 5 minutes or until just tender. Refrigerate pears several hours, turning pears occasionally to coat with syrup.

3 Remove pears from syrup; strain 3/4 cup (180ml) syrup into small microwave-safe bowl. Stir in extra sugar and cornflour blended with extra water; cook, uncovered, on HIGH (100%) about 3 minutes or until sauce boils and thickens, whisking once during cooking. Cool. Serve pears with syrup and cinnamon cream.

Cinnamon cream Beat all ingredients in small bowl with electric mixer until soft peaks form.

SERVES 4

per serve 27.8g fat; 2172kJ

apple and pear crumble

PREPARATION TIME 25 MINUTES • COOKING TIME 12 MINUTES

3 large (600g) apples, peeled, cored, sliced
3 small (540g) pears, peeled, cored, sliced
1 tablespoon caster sugar
1 tablespoon honey

CRUMBLE TOPPING

1/2 cup (75g) self-raising flour
1 teaspoon ground cinnamon
3/4 cup (65g) rolled oats
1/3 cup (30g) desiccated coconut
75g cold butter
1/3 cup (75g) firmly packed brown sugar

1 Place apple, pear, sugar and honey in shallow 2-litre (8-cup) microwave-safe dish; cook, covered, on HIGH (100%) about 5 minutes or until fruit is just tender, stirring once during cooking.

2 Sprinkle with crumble topping; cook, uncovered, on HIGH (100%) about 6 minutes or until topping is firm.

Crumble topping Combine flour, cinnamon, oats and coconut in bowl; rub in butter, stir in sugar.

SERVES 4

per serve 22.2g fat; 2212kJ

moist carrot cake

PREPARATION TIME 25 MINUTES (PLUS COOLING TIME) • COOKING TIME 15 MINUTES

You will need about 4 medium (480g) carrots for this recipe.

1 cup (150g) self-raising flour
3/4 cup (150g) firmly packed brown sugar
2 teaspoons ground cinnamon
2 cups coarsely grated carrot
1/2 cup (85g) chopped raisins
1/2 cup (125ml) vegetable oil
2 eggs
1/3 cup (40g) chopped walnuts

FROSTING

60g packaged cream cheese
30g butter
1 1/2 cups (240g) icing sugar mixture
2 teaspoons lemon juice

1. Grease 21cm microwave-safe ring pan, line base with baking paper.
2. Combine flour, sugar, cinnamon, carrot and raisins in large bowl; stir in oil and eggs.
3. Pour mixture into prepared pan; cook, uncovered, on MEDIUM-HIGH (70%) about 10 minutes or until just cooked. Stand cake 5 minutes before turning onto wire rack to cool. Top with frosting and walnuts.

Frosting Beat cream cheese and butter in small bowl with electric mixer until smooth; gradually add icing sugar and juice, beat until combined.

SERVES 8

per serve 26g fat; 2231kJ

lemon delicious

PREPARATION TIME 20 MINUTES • COOKING TIME 10 MINUTES

2 egg yolks
1/2 cup (110g) caster sugar
2 teaspoons grated lemon rind
1/3 cup (50g) self-raising flour
1 teaspoon ground ginger
1/4 cup (60ml) lemon juice
3/4 cup (180ml) milk
40g butter, melted
3 egg whites

1 Grease deep 1-litre (4-cup) microwave-safe dish.

2 Beat egg yolks, sugar and rind in small bowl with electric mixer until thick and creamy. Gently fold in flour and ginger, then juice, milk and butter.

3 Beat egg whites in small bowl with electric mixer until soft peaks form; fold into lemon mixture in 2 batches.

4 Spoon into prepared dish; cook, uncovered, on MEDIUM-HIGH (70%) about 5 minutes or until centre is almost set. Stand 5 minutes. Dust with sifted icing sugar, if desired.

SERVES 4

per serve 13.5g fat; 1265kJ

easy christmas pudding

PREPARATION TIME 20 MINUTES • COOKING TIME 35 MINUTES

Parisian essence is a flavourless liquid used to give food a brown colour, but it is not essential in making this pudding.

2¾ cups (500g) mixed dried fruit
⅓ cup (80ml) brandy or orange juice
125g butter, softened
¾ cup (150g) firmly packed brown sugar
2 tablespoons golden syrup
2 eggs
1 teaspoon Parisian essence
1 large (200g) apple, peeled, cored, grated
¾ cup (110g) plain flour
2 teaspoons mixed spice
½ teaspoon bicarbonate of soda

1 Grease 2.5-litre (10-cup) microwave-safe bowl, line base with baking paper.

2 Combine fruit and brandy in another large microwave-safe bowl; cook, covered, on HIGH (100%) 1 minute, cool slightly.

3 Beat butter, sugar and syrup in small bowl with electric mixer until just combined. Beat in eggs, 1 at a time. Add to fruit mixture with essence, apple and sifted dry ingredients. Spoon mixture into prepared bowl; smooth top.

4 Cook, uncovered, on MEDIUM (55%) 10 minutes. Rotate bowl 180 degrees; cook, uncovered, on MEDIUM (55%) about 10 minutes or until centre of pudding is almost cooked. Stand, covered, 15 minutes before turning onto serving plate.

SERVES 8

per serve 15.3g fat; 1968kJ

one-bowl chocolate cake

PREPARATION TIME 20 MINUTES (PLUS REFRIGERATION TIME) • COOKING TIME 20 MINUTES

125g butter
1 cup (220g) caster sugar
1 cup (250ml) water
1½ cups (225g) self-raising flour
⅓ cup (35g) cocoa
½ teaspoon bicarbonate of soda
2 eggs, beaten lightly

FUDGE FROSTING

45g butter
2 tablespoons water
¼ cup (55g) caster sugar
¾ cup (120g) icing sugar mixture
2 tablespoons cocoa

1 Grease 21cm microwave-safe ring pan, line with baking paper.
2 Combine butter, sugar and the water in large microwave-safe bowl; cook, uncovered, on HIGH (100%) 4 minutes, stirring once during cooking. Cool to room temperature.
3 Sift dry ingredients into butter mixture; whisk mixture until smooth, stir in egg.
4 Pour mixture into prepared pan; cook, uncovered, on MEDIUM-HIGH (70%) about 10 minutes or until just cooked. Stand 5 minutes before turning onto wire rack to cool.
5 Spread with fudge frosting.

Fudge frosting Combine butter, the water and caster sugar in small microwave-safe bowl; cook, uncovered, on HIGH (100%) 1 minute, stir until sugar dissolves. Whisk in sifted icing sugar and cocoa. Cover; refrigerate 30 minutes or until frosting thickens. Beat until a spreadable consistency.

SERVES 8

per serve 20.3g fat; 2007kJ

preserves

Jams, jellies, chutneys, pickles, savoury sauces and relishes can all be made in the microwave oven with great success – it's an easy and timesaving way to keep the best of the season's produce ready to eat all the rest of the year. Here are a few important rules to follow...

tips for making preserves

- As a guide, do not use more than 500g of fruit and vegetables for each recipe, as small quantities work best in the microwave oven.
- Since there is a minimal amount of evaporation of liquid during cooking in the microwave oven, there is generally less liquid used in recipes than in conventional recipes.
- Always use a large shallow microwave-safe dish for cooking preserves, and check the preserve often during cooking time; stir gently to check consistency.
- Cover preserves during cooking only when specified.
- After the minimum suggested cooking time, open the oven door and allow bubbles to subside. Drop a teaspoon of the preserve onto a cold plate; cool to room temperature. If the cooled preserve is the consistency you're after, it is ready to bottle. If not, continue to cook.
- Cooking times given in recipes are a guide only; times vary depending on the type of oven and utensils used, as well as on the ripeness and water content of the fruit and vegetables.
- All fruit – especially citrus rinds – must be softened before adding sugar. Sugar must be dissolved before the mixture boils.
- Butters, spreads and curds based on butter and/or eggs require careful monitoring during cooking; they will curdle and separate if they are allowed to boil.
- All preserves must be poured, while hot, into hot sterilised jars or bottles; seal immediately.
- Follow individual recipes for storage times. Always store opened jars or bottles, covered, in the refrigerator. Unopened jars or bottles can be stored in the pantry but, if you live in a humid climate, the refrigerator is the best place to store preserves.
- Sterilise jars and bottles by placing them and their metal lids in a large pan filled with cold water; cover, turn heat to maximum. When water boils, remove pan lid; boil 20 minutes. Using oven mitts and kitchen tongs, remove jars and lids from pan; drain excess water from jars, stand upright to allow any remaining water to evaporate. You can also wash jars in your dishwasher without detergent. It is important to use jars while they are hot and to seal them while still hot.

tangy strawberry jam *(recipe on page 108)*

apricot citrus marmalade

PREPARATION TIME 25 MINUTES (PLUS STANDING TIME) • **COOKING TIME** 30 MINUTES

1 medium (180g) orange
1 large (180g) lemon
1 tablespoon water
3/4 cup (110g) dried apricots
2 cups (500ml) water, extra
2 1/2 cups (550g) caster sugar, approximately

1. Remove and reserve seeds from unpeeled quartered orange and lemon. Put seeds and the 1 tablespoon water in small bowl; cover, stand overnight.
2. Roughly chop orange, lemon and apricots; blend or process until finely chopped. Combine fruit with the 2 cups extra water in large glass microwave-safe bowl.
3. Cook, covered, on HIGH (100%) about 20 minutes or until rind is soft, stirring once during cooking. Do not uncover; stand fruit mixture overnight.
4. Next day, drain seeds over fruit mixture; discard seeds.
5. Measure fruit mixture; allow 1 cup (220g) sugar for every 1 cup fruit mixture. Return fruit mixture and sugar to same bowl; cook, uncovered, on HIGH (100%) 5 minutes, stirring twice during cooking.
6. Cook, uncovered, without stirring, on HIGH (100%) about 5 minutes or until marmalade jells when tested. Skim surface, pour into hot sterilised jars; seal while hot.

MAKES ABOUT 3 1/2 CUPS (875ml)

storage refrigerated for 2 months
per serve 0g fat; 121kJ

peach and passionfruit jam

PREPARATION TIME 30 MINUTES (PLUS STANDING TIME) • **COOKING TIME** 1 HOUR

You will need about 8 passionfruit for this recipe.

1 medium (180g) orange
1 medium (140g) lemon
2 tablespoons water
1 cup (250ml) water, extra
5 medium (1kg) peaches, peeled, sliced thinly
4 cups (880g) caster sugar, approximately
2/3 cup (160ml) passionfruit pulp

1 Remove and reserve seeds from unpeeled roughly chopped orange and lemon. Put seeds and the 2 tablepoons water in small bowl; cover, stand mixture overnight.

2 Blend or process orange and lemon until finely chopped. Combine fruit mixture with the 1 cup extra water in large glass microwave-safe bowl, cover; stand overnight.

3 Next day, drain seeds over fruit mixture; discard seeds.

4 Cook, covered, on HIGH (100%) 15 minutes, stirring once during cooking. Add peaches; cook, uncovered, on HIGH (100%) about 10 minutes or until peaches are soft and pulpy, stirring once during cooking.

5 Measure fruit mixture; allow 1 cup (220g) sugar for every 1 cup fruit mixture. Return fruit mixture and sugar to same bowl, stir until sugar dissolves.

6 Cook, uncovered, on HIGH (100%) about 25 minutes or until jam jells when tested, stirring 3 times during cooking. Skim surface; gently stir in passionfruit pulp; stand 5 minutes. Pour into hot sterilised jars; seal while hot.

MAKES ABOUT 5 CUPS (1.25 litres)

storage refrigerated for 2 months
per serve 0g fat; 133kJ

fruit jams made in minutes

PREPARATION TIME 15 MINUTES • COOKING TIME 20 TO 35 MINUTES

rhubarb berry jam

4 cups (440g) chopped rhubarb
500g fresh or frozen blackberries
1 teaspoon finely grated orange rind
1 tablespoon orange juice
1 tablespoon lemon juice
1¾ cups (385g) caster sugar

1. Combine rhubarb, berries, rind and juices in large glass microwave-safe bowl; cook, uncovered, on HIGH (100%) 10 minutes, stirring once during cooking.
2. Add sugar, stir until sugar dissolves. Cook, uncovered, on HIGH (100%) about 20 minutes or until jam jells when tested, stirring 3 times during cooking. Pour into hot sterilised jars; seal while hot.

MAKES ABOUT 3 CUPS (750ml)

storage refrigerated for 2 months
per serve 0g fat; 100kJ

tomato and apple

4 medium (750g) tomatoes, peeled
1 small (130g) apple, peeled, grated coarsely
⅓ cup (75g) finely chopped glacé ginger
¼ cup (60ml) lemon juice
2 cups (440g) caster sugar

1. Roughly chop tomatoes, combine with apple and ginger in large glass microwave-safe bowl; cook, uncovered, on HIGH (100%) about 15 minutes or until mixture is pulpy.
2. Add juice and sugar, stir until sugar dissolves. Cook, uncovered, on HIGH (100%) about 20 minutes or until jam jells when tested, stirring 3 times during cooking. Pour into hot sterilised jars; seal while hot.

MAKES ABOUT 2½ CUPS (625ml)

storage refrigerated for 2 months
per serve 0g fat; 146kJ

apricot and passionfruit

You will need about 6 passionfruit for this recipe.

3⅓ cups (500g) dried apricots, halved
¼ cup (60ml) lemon juice
2 cups (500ml) water
4 cups (880g) caster sugar
½ cup (125ml) passionfruit pulp

1. Combine apricots, juice and the water in large glass microwave-safe bowl; cook, uncovered, on HIGH (100%) 15 minutes, stirring once during cooking.
2. Add sugar, stir until sugar dissolves. Cook, uncovered, on HIGH (100%) about 10 minutes or until jam jells when tested, stirring 3 times during cooking.
3. Add passionfruit pulp; stand 2 minutes, stir jam to distribute seeds. Pour into hot sterilised jars; seal while hot.

MAKES ABOUT 5 CUPS (1.25 litres)

storage refrigerated for 2 months
per serve 0g fat; 154kJ

tangy strawberry

Grand Marnier is an orange-flavoured liqueur. You can substitute Cointreau or Triple Sec, if desired.

500g strawberries, hulled, quartered
¼ cup (60ml) lemon juice
2 cups (440g) caster sugar
2 tablespoons Grand Marnier

1. Cook strawberries and juice in large glass microwave-safe bowl, uncovered, on HIGH (100%) 5 minutes. Add sugar, stir until sugar dissolves.
2. Cook, uncovered, on HIGH (100%) about 15 minutes or until jam jells when tested, stirring 3 times during cooking. Stir in liqueur. Pour into hot sterilised jars; seal while hot.

MAKES ABOUT 1½ CUPS (375ml)

storage refrigerated for 2 months
per serve 0g fat; 224kJ

Rhubarb Berry Jam

sweet chilli tomato sauce

PREPARATION TIME 25 MINUTES • **COOKING TIME** 25 MINUTES

4 large (1kg) tomatoes, peeled, chopped
1 teaspoon salt
4 cloves garlic, chopped
1/4 cup (60ml) balsamic vinegar
1/4 cup (55g) sugar
1/4 cup chopped fresh coriander leaves
3 small fresh red chillies, chopped

1. Combine all ingredients in large glass microwave-safe bowl. Cook, uncovered, on HIGH (100%) about 25 minutes or until sauce thickens, stirring twice during cooking; cool 5 minutes.
2. Blend or process sauce until smooth. Pour into hot sterilised bottles; seal while hot.

MAKES ABOUT 2 1/2 CUPS (625ml)

storage refrigerated for 2 weeks
per serve 0g fat; 25kJ

citrus butter

PREPARATION TIME 25 MINUTES • COOKING TIME 10 MINUTES

4 eggs
3/4 cup (165g) sugar
1 teaspoon finely grated lemon rind
1/4 cup (60ml) lemon juice
1 teaspoon finely grated orange rind
1/4 cup (60ml) orange juice
1/4 cup (60ml) water
125g unsalted butter, chopped

1 Whisk eggs and sugar together in large glass microwave-safe bowl; gently stir in remaining ingredients.

2 Cook butter mixture, uncovered, on MEDIUM (55%) 6 minutes, whisking every 2 minutes.

3 Cook mixture, uncovered, on MEDIUM (55%) about 2 minutes or until it thickens, whisking once during cooking. Pour into hot sterilised jars; seal while hot.

MAKES ABOUT 2 CUPS (500ml)

storage refrigerated for 1 month
per serve 2.5g fat; 164kJ

green tomato relish

PREPARATION TIME 20 MINUTES

COOKING TIME 1 HOUR 20 MINUTES

6 large (1.5kg) green tomatoes, chopped
2 medium (300g) brown onions, chopped
2 cloves garlic, crushed
1 cup (250ml) cider vinegar
1/4 cup (60ml) brown malt vinegar
1 cup (220g) sugar
2 teaspoons salt
1 teaspoon ground ginger
4 cloves
1/2 teaspoon ground cardamom
1/2 teaspoon ground cinnamon
1/2 teaspoon ground turmeric

1 Combine all ingredients in large glass microwave-safe bowl; cook, uncovered, on HIGH (100%) about 5 minutes or until sugar dissolves, stirring 3 times during cooking.
2 Cook relish, uncovered, on HIGH (100%) about 1 1/4 hours or until mixture thickens, stirring 3 times during cooking.
3 Spoon into hot sterilised jars; seal while hot.

MAKES ABOUT 4 CUPS (1 litre)

storage refrigerated for 2 months
per serve 0g fat; 52kJ

spicy onion and tomato relish

PREPARATION TIME 30 MINUTES

COOKING TIME 1 HOUR

6 medium (1.1kg) tomatoes, chopped
2 medium (300g) onions, chopped finely
2 medium (300g) apples, peeled, chopped finely
1 teaspoon salt
1 teaspoon finely grated lemon rind
1 teaspoon dry mustard
1 teaspoon garam masala
2 tablespoons mild curry powder
1 1/4 cups (250g) firmly packed brown sugar
1/2 cup (125ml) white vinegar
1/4 cup (60ml) lemon juice
1 tablespoon tomato paste

1 Combine all ingredients in large glass microwave-safe bowl; cook, uncovered, on HIGH (100%) about 1 hour or until mixture thickens, stirring 3 times during cooking.
2 Spoon into hot sterilised jars; seal while hot.

MAKES ABOUT 4 CUPS (1 litre)

storage refrigerated for 2 months
per serve 0g fat; 62kJ

dried fruit chutney *(top)*
green tomato relish *(centre)*
spicy onion and tomato relish *(right)*

dried fruit chutney

PREPARATION TIME 25 MINUTES
COOKING TIME 50 MINUTES

1 1/3 cups (200g) chopped dried pears
1 1/3 cups (200g) chopped dried apricots
1 1/4 cups (200g) chopped seeded dates
2 cups (180g) chopped dried apples
1 1/2 cups (240g) sultanas
2 cups (500ml) water
2 cups (400g) firmly packed brown sugar
2 cups (500ml) cider vinegar
1/2 teaspoon chilli powder
1/2 teaspoon ground turmeric
1/2 teaspoon ground nutmeg
1/2 teaspoon ground ginger
1 clove garlic, crushed

1 Combine dried fruits with the water in large glass microwave-safe bowl; cook, covered, on HIGH (100%) 10 minutes, stirring once during cooking. Stand, covered, 10 minutes. Add sugar, stir until sugar dissolves.
2 Add remaining ingredients; cook, uncovered, on HIGH (100%) about 30 minutes or until mixture is thick, stirring 3 times during cooking.
3 Spoon into hot sterilised jars; seal while hot.

MAKES ABOUT 7 CUPS
(1.75 litres)

storage refrigerated for 2 months
per serve 0g fat; 105kJ

glossary

Bacon rashers Also known as slices of bacon; made from pork side, cured and smoked. Streaky bacon is the fatty end of a bacon rasher (slice), without the lean (eye) meat.

Bamboo shoots The tender young shoots of bamboo plants, available fresh from Asian food stores or specialty greengrocers, or canned.

Beans

BUTTER Another name for dried lima beans, sold both in dried and canned versions; a large off-white bean with a mealy texture and sweet flavour.

REFRIED Similar to borlotti beans, cooked twice, soaked and boiled then mashed and fried, traditionally in lard. A Mexican staple, "frijoles refritos" or refried beans are available canned in supermarkets. Mexe-Beans is the trade name for a canned pinto bean in chilli sauce mixture.

Bean sprouts Also known as bean shoots; tender new growths of assorted beans and seeds germinated for consumption as sprouts. The most readily available are mung bean, soy bean, alfalfa and snow pea sprouts.

Beef, minced Also known as ground beef.

Bicarbonate of soda Also known as baking soda.

Biscuit crumbs Crushed plain, un-iced biscuits (cookies) used in making cheesecake crusts and other desserts.

Bok choy Also called pak choi or Chinese white cabbage; has a fresh, mild mustard taste and is good braised or in stir-fries. Baby bok choy is also available. It is tender and more delicate in flavour.

Breadcrumbs

PACKAGED Fine-textured, crunchy, purchased, white breadcrumbs.

STALE 1- or 2-day-old bread made into crumbs by grating, blending or processing.

Broccoli A green vegetable, member of cabbage family, usually cut into florets before using.

Butter Use salted or unsalted ("sweet") butter; 125g is equal to 1 stick butter.

Cajun seasoning Used to give an authentic USA Deep South spicy Cajun flavour to food. This packaged blend of assorted herbs and spices can include paprika, basil, onion, fennel, thyme, cayenne and tarragon.

Capsicum Also known as bell pepper or, simply, pepper, available in red, green, yellow and deep-purple varieties, each with a distinctive taste. Seeds and membranes should be discarded before use.

Cayenne pepper A thin-fleshed, long, extremely hot red chilli; usually purchased dried and ground.

Cheese

CHEDDAR The most common cow milk "tasty" cheese; should be aged, hard and have a pronounced bite flavour. (Fat: 6.7g per 20g serving.)

CREAM Commonly known as "Philadelphia" or "Philly", a soft milk cheese having no less than 33% butterfat. (Fat: 6.7g per 20g serving.)

FETTA Greek in origin; a crumbly textured goat or sheep milk cheese with a sharp, salty taste. (Fat: 5g per 20g serving.)

MOZZARELLA A semi-soft cheese with a delicate, fresh taste; has a low melting point and stringy texture when heated. (Fat: 4.6g per 20g serving.)

PARMESAN A sharp-tasting, dry, hard cheese, made from skim or part-skim milk and aged for at least a year before being sold. Parmigiano Reggiano, from Italy, aged a minimum three years, is one of the best. (Fat: 6.3g per 20g serving.)

PIZZA CHEESE A commercial blend of varying proportions of processed grated mozzarella, cheddar and parmesan. (Fat: 4.3g per 20g serving.)

Chickpeas Also called garbanzos, hummus or channa; an irregularly round, sandy-coloured legume used extensively in Mediterranean and Latin cooking.

Chillies Available in many different types and sizes, both fresh and dried. Generally the smaller the chilli, the hotter it is. Use rubber gloves when seeding and chopping fresh chillies as they can burn your skin. Removing seeds and membranes lessens the heat level.

CHILLI SAUCE Our recipes use a hot Chinese variety made of chillies, salt and vinegar; use sparingly, increasing amounts to taste. Sweet Chilli Sauce is a comparatively mild, Thai-style sauce made from red chillies, sugar, garlic and vinegar.

Chinese broccoli Also known as gai lum.

Chives Related to the onion and leek, with subtle onion flavour. Chives and flowering chives are interchangeable.

chinese broccoli
water chestnuts
bok choy
bean sprouts

GARLIC CHIVES have flat leaves and a stronger flavour than chives.

Chocolate, dark Eating chocolate; made of cocoa liquor, cocoa butter and sugar.

Choko Also known as chayote or christophene. A pear-shaped vegetable with pale green skin.

Cocoa Cocoa powder.

Coconut

CREAM Available in cans and cartons; as a rule the proportions are 4 parts coconut to 1 part water.

MILK Pure, unsweetened coconut milk is available in cans and cartons; as a rule, the proportions are 2 parts coconut to 1 part water.

Corn chips Packaged snack food that evolved from fried corn tortilla pieces.

Corn

CREAMED Available in cans from most supermarkets.

FLAKE CRUMBS A packaged product of crushed Corn Flakes used to coat chicken etc.

FLAKES Crisp flakes made from toasted corn. A universally popular breakfast cereal.

FLOUR Also known as cornstarch; used as a thickening agent in cooking.

fetta
cheddar
mozzarella
pizza cheese
parmesan
cream cheese

MEAL Ground, dried corn (maize); similar to polenta but slightly coarser. One can be substituted for the other, but textures will vary.

Couscous A fine, grain-like cereal product, originally from North Africa; made from semolina.

Cream

FRESH Also known as pure cream and pouring cream (minimum fat content 35%); has no additives like commercially thickened cream.

SOUR A thick, commercially-cultured soured cream (minimum fat content 35%); good for dips, toppings and baked cheesecakes.

THICKENED A whipping cream (minimum fat content 35%) containing a thickener such as gelatine.

Csabai sausage Hungarian in origin, a dried pork or beef sausage flavoured with pimiento, paprika and cracked black peppercorns.

Eggplant Also known as aubergine.

Essences Also known as extracts; generally the by-product of distillation of plants.

Fish sauce Also called nam pla or nuoc nam; made from pulverised, salted, fermented fish, most often anchovies. Has a pungent smell and strong taste; use sparingly. There are many kinds, of varying intensity.

Five-spice powder A fragrant mixture of ground cinnamon, cloves, star anise, Sichuan pepper and fennel seeds.

Flour

PLAIN An all-purpose flour, made from wheat.

SELF-RAISING Plain flour sifted with baking powder in the proportion of 1 cup flour to 2 teaspoons baking powder.

WHOLEMEAL SELF-RAISING Wholemeal flour (also called whole-wheat flour) with baking powder and salt added.

Garam masala A blend of spices, originating in North India; based on varying proportions of cardamom, cinnamon, cloves, coriander, fennel and cumin, roasted and ground together. Black pepper and chilli can be added for a hotter version.

Gelatine (gelatin) We used powdered gelatine. It is also available in sheet form, known as leaf gelatine.

Ghee Clarified butter; with the milk solids removed, this fat can be heated to a high temperature without burning.

Gherkin Sometimes known as a cornichon; both the name of a tiny, dark-green cucumber and the term to describe it after it has been pickled with herbs and vinegar.

Ginger

FRESH Also known as green or root ginger; the gnarled root of a tropical plant. Can be kept, peeled, covered with dry sherry in a jar and refrigerated, or frozen in an airtight container.

GLACE Fresh ginger root preserved in sugar syrup. Crystallised ginger can be substituted if rinsed with warm water and dried before using.

GROUND Also known as powdered ginger; used as a flavouring in cakes, pies and puddings but cannot be substituted for fresh ginger.

Golden syrup A by-product of refined sugarcane; pure maple syrup or honey can be substituted.

Gow gee pastry rounds Wonton wrappers, spring roll or egg pastry sheets can be substituted.

Herbs We have specified when to use fresh or dried herbs. To substitute dried for fresh herbs, use in the ratio of 1:4 for fresh herbs; e.g. 1 teaspoon dried herbs equals 4 teaspoons chopped fresh herbs.

Hoisin sauce A thick, sweet and spicy Chinese paste made from salted, fermented soy beans, onions and garlic; used as a marinade or baste, or to accent stir-fries and barbecued or roasted foods.

Jam Also known as preserve or conserve; most often made from fruit.

Kumara Polynesian name of orange-fleshed sweet potato, often confused with yam.

Lamb

FILLET Tenderloin; the smaller piece of meat from a row of loin chops or cutlets.

MINCE Also known as ground lamb.

RACK Row of cutlets.

Maple-flavoured syrup Also known as golden or pancake syrup, it is made from cane sugar and artificial maple flavouring; not the same as pure maple syrup.

Marinara seafood mix A mixture of uncooked chopped seafood available from fishmarkets and fishmongers.

Milk We used full-cream homogenised milk unless otherwise specified.

SWEETENED CONDENSED A canned milk product consisting of milk with more than half the water content removed and sugar added to the milk which remains.

Mint jelly A condiment usually served with roast lamb; packaged or homemade jelly flavoured with mint flakes.

Mixed dried fruit A combination of sultanas, raisins, currants, mixed peel and cherries.

Mixed spice A blend of ground spices usually consisting of cinnamon, allspice and nutmeg.

Mushrooms

BUTTON Small, cultivated white mushrooms having a delicate, subtle flavour.

FIELD Very similar to flat mushrooms but with darker, flatter tops.

DRIED SHIITAKE Also known as donko or dried Chinese mushrooms; have a unique meaty flavour.

OYSTER (ABALONE) Grey-white mushroom shaped like a fan.

SWISS BROWN Light to dark brown mushrooms with full-bodied flavour. Button or cup mushrooms can be substituted for Swiss brown mushrooms.

Mustard, seeded Also known as wholegrain. A French-style coarse-grain mustard made from crushed mustard seeds and Dijon mustard.

Noodles

BEAN THREAD Also called cellophane noodles; made from green mung bean flour. Good in soups and salads.

FRESH CHOW MEIN These are becoming easier to obtain, with large supermarkets now stocking them. Substitute fresh wheat noodles, commonly labelled Hokkien or stir-fry noodles, if you cannot find fresh chow mein.

FRESH EGG Made from wheat flour and eggs; strands vary in thickness.

Oil

OLIVE Extra virgin and virgin: the highest quality olive oils, from the first pressings of the olives. Mono-unsaturated: made from the pressing of tree-ripened olives. Especially good for everyday cooking and in salad dressings. Extra Light or Light: describes the mild flavour, not the fat levels.

PEANUT Pressed from ground peanuts; most commonly used oil in Asian cooking because of its high smoke point.

SESAME Made from roasted, crushed, white sesame seeds; a flavouring rather than a cooking medium.

VEGETABLE Any of a number of oils sourced from plants rather than animal fats.

Onion

GREEN Also known as scallion or (incorrectly) shallot; an immature onion picked before the bulb has formed, having a long, bright-green edible stalk.

SPRING Have crisp, narrow, green-leafed tops and a fairly large, sweet white bulb.

Oyster sauce Asian in origin, this rich, brown sauce is made from oysters and their brine, cooked with salt and soy sauce, and thickened with starches.

field mushroom

dried shiitake mushrooms

button mushrooms

swiss brown mushrooms

oyster mushrooms

Paprika Ground, dried red capsicum (bell pepper), available sweet or hot.

Passionfruit Also known as granadilla; a small tropical fruit, native to Brazil, comprised of a tough outer skin surrounding edible black sweet-sour seeds.

Plum sauce A thick, sweet and sour dipping sauce made from plums, vinegar, sugar, chillies and spices.

Polenta A flour-like cereal made of ground corn (maize); similar to cornmeal but coarser and darker in colour. Also the name of the dish made from it.

Pork

CHINESE BARBECUE Also known as char siew. Traditionally cooked in special ovens, this pork has a sweet-sticky coating made from soy sauce, sherry, five-spice and hoisin sauce. It is available from Asian food stores.

FILLET Skinless, boneless eye-fillet cut from the loin.

PORK AND VEAL MINCE A combination of finely ground fresh pork and veal.

Prawns Also known as shrimp.

Prunes Commercially- or sun-dried plums.

Rice

ARBORIO Small, round-grain rice well-suited to absorb a large amount of liquid; especially suitable for risottos.

BASMATI A fragrant, long-grained white rice. It should be washed several times to remove grit before cooking.

BROWN Natural whole grain. It is the entire grain having had the outer husk discarded.

CALROSE A medium-grain rice that is extremely versatile; can be substituted for short- or long-grain rices if necessary.

WHITE LONG GRAIN Elongated grain, remains separate when cooked; most popular steaming rice in Asia.

Rolled oats Whole oat grains husked, steam-softened, flattened with rollers, dried and packaged for consumption as a cereal product.

Rum, dark We prefer to use an underproof rum (not overproof) for a more subtle flavour.

Salsa, bottled A combination of tomatoes, onions, peppers, vinegar, herbs and spices.

Sambal oelek (also ulek or olek) Indonesian in origin; a salty paste made from ground chillies, sugar and spices.

Seasoned pepper A packaged preparation of combined black pepper, red capsicum (bell pepper), paprika and garlic.

Sesame seeds Black and white are the most common of the oval seeds harvested from the tropical plant *Sesamum indicum*; however there are red and brown varieties also. Used in halva and tahini; are a good source of calcium. To toast, stir in a dry pan over medium heat until fragrant.

Snow peas Also called mange tout ("eat all").

Spinach English spinach is the correct name for spinach; the green vegetable often called spinach is correctly known as Swiss chard, silverbeet or seakale. Delicate, green leaves on thin stems; high in iron, it's good eaten raw in salads or steamed gently on its own.

Stock 1 cup (250ml) stock is the equivalent of 1 cup (250ml) water plus 1 crumbled stock cube (or 1 teaspoon stock powder). If you prefer to make your own fresh stock, see recipes on page 118.

Sugar

We used coarse, granulated table sugar, also known as crystal sugar, unless otherwise specified.

BROWN An extremely soft, fine granulated sugar retaining molasses for its characteristic colour and flavour.

CASTER Also known as superfine or finely granulated table sugar.

ICING SUGAR MIXTURE Also known as confectioners' sugar or powdered sugar; granulated sugar crushed together with a small amount (about 3%) cornflour added.

RAW Natural brown granulated sugar.

Sultanas Golden raisins.

Tabasco sauce Brand name of an extremely fiery sauce made from vinegar, hot red peppers and salt.

Tahini A rich, buttery paste made from crushed sesame seeds; used in making hummus and other Middle-Eastern sauces.

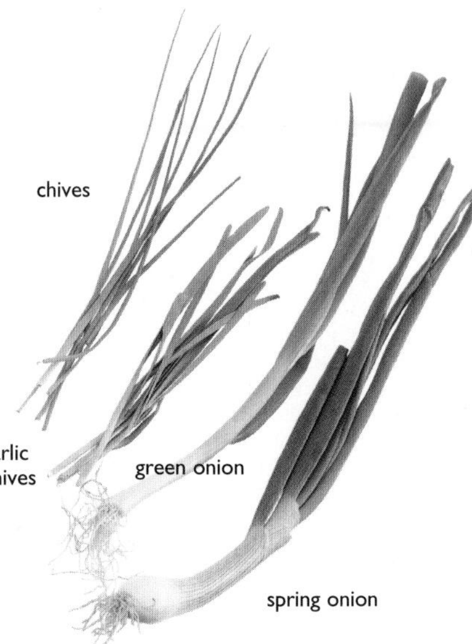

Tomato

PASTE Triple-concentrated tomato puree used to flavour soups, stews, sauces and casseroles.

PUREE Canned, pureed tomatoes (not tomato paste). Substitute with fresh peeled and pureed tomatoes.

SAUCE Also known as ketchup or catsup; a flavoured condiment made from slow-cooked tomatoes, vinegar and spices.

SUPREME A canned product consisting of tomatoes, onions, celery, peppers, cheese and seasonings.

Vinegar, balsamic Authentic only from the province of Modena, Italy; made from a regional wine of white Trebbiano grapes specially processed then aged in antique wooden casks to give it its uniquely exquisite, pungent flavour.

Water chestnuts Resemble chestnuts in appearance, hence the English name. They are small brown tubers with a crisp, white, nutty-tasting flesh. Their crunchy texture is best experienced fresh, however canned water chestnuts are more easily obtained and can be kept about a month, once opened, under refrigeration.

Yogurt Plain, unflavoured yogurt – in addition to being good eaten on its own – can be used as a meat tenderiser, as the basis for various sauces and dips or as an enricher and thickener.

Zucchini Also known as courgette.

index

make your own stock

These recipes can be made up to 4 days ahead and stored, covered, in the refrigerator. Be sure to remove any fat from the surface after the cooled stock has been refrigerated overnight. If the stock is to be kept longer, it is best to freeze it in smaller quantities. *All stock recipes make about 2.5 litres (10 cups).*

Stock is also available in cans or tetra packs. Stock cubes or powder can be used. As a guide, 1 teaspoon of stock powder or 1 small crumbled stock cube mixed with 1 cup (250ml) water will give a fairly strong stock. Be aware of the salt and fat content of stock cubes and powders and prepared stocks.

BEEF STOCK

2kg meaty beef bones
2 medium (300g) onions
2 sticks celery, chopped
2 medium (250g) carrots, chopped
3 bay leaves
2 teaspoons black peppercorns
5 litres (20 cups) water
3 litres (12 cups) water, extra

Place bones and unpeeled chopped onions in baking dish. Bake in hot oven about 1 hour or until bones and onions are well browned. Transfer bones and onions to large pan, add celery, carrots, bay leaves, peppercorns and water, simmer, uncovered, 3 hours. Add extra water, simmer, uncovered, further 1 hour; strain.

CHICKEN STOCK

2kg chicken bones
2 medium (300g) onions, chopped
2 sticks celery, chopped
2 medium (250g) carrots, chopped
3 bay leaves
2 teaspoons black peppercorns
5 litres (20 cups) water

Combine all ingredients in large pan, simmer, uncovered, 2 hours; strain.

FISH STOCK

1.5kg fish bones
3 litres (12 cups) water
1 medium (150g) onion, chopped
2 sticks celery, chopped
2 bay leaves
1 teaspoon black peppercorns

Combine all ingredients in large pan, simmer, uncovered, 20 minutes; strain.

VEGETABLE STOCK

2 large (360g) carrots, chopped
2 large (360g) parsnips, chopped
4 medium (600g) onions, chopped
12 sticks celery, chopped
4 bay leaves
2 teaspoons black peppercorns
6 litres (24 cups) water

Combine all ingredients in large pan, simmer, uncovered, 1 1/2 hours; strain.

facts and figures

Wherever you live, you'll be able to use our recipes with the help of these easy-to-follow conversions. While these conversions are approximate only, the difference between an exact and the approximate conversion of various liquid and dry measures is minimal and will not affect your cooking results.

dry measures

metric	imperial
15g	1/2oz
30g	1oz
60g	2oz
90g	3oz
125g	4oz (1/4lb)
155g	5oz
185g	6oz
220g	7oz
250g	8oz (1/2lb)
280g	9oz
315g	10oz
345g	11oz
375g	12oz (3/4lb)
410g	13oz
440g	14oz
470g	15oz
500g	16oz (1lb)
750g	24oz (1 1/2lb)
1kg	32oz (2lb)

liquid measures

metric	imperial
30ml	1 fluid oz
60ml	2 fluid oz
100ml	3 fluid oz
125ml	4 fluid oz
150ml	5 fluid oz (1/4 pint/1 gill)
190ml	6 fluid oz
250ml	8 fluid oz
300ml	10 fluid oz (1/2 pint)
500ml	16 fluid oz
600ml	20 fluid oz (1 pint)
1 litre	32 fluid oz (1 3/4 pints)

helpful measures

metric	imperial
3mm	1/8in
6mm	1/4in
1cm	1/2in
2cm	3/4in
2.5cm	1in
5cm	2in
6cm	2 1/2in
8cm	3in
10cm	4in
13cm	5in
15cm	6in
18cm	7in
20cm	8in
23cm	9in
25cm	10in
28cm	11in
30cm	12in (1ft)

measuring equipment

The difference between one country's measuring cups and another's varies, at the most, by 2 or 3 teaspoons. (For the record, 1 Australian metric measuring cup holds approximately 250ml.) The most accurate way of measuring dry ingredients is to weigh them. When measuring liquids, use a clear glass or plastic jug with metric markings. (One Australian metric tablespoon holds 20ml; one Australian metric teaspoon holds 5ml.)

If you would like to purchase *The Australian Women's Weekly* Test Kitchen's metric measuring cups and spoons (as approved by Standards Australia), turn to page 120 for details and order coupon. You will receive:

- a graduated set of 4 cups for measuring dry ingredients, with sizes marked on the cups.
- a graduated set of 4 spoons for measuring dry and liquid ingredients, with amounts marked on the spoons.

Note: North America, New Zealand and the UK use 15ml tablespoons. All cup and spoon measurements are level.

We use large eggs having an average weight of 60g.

microwave oven temperatures

Power levels vary between microwave ovens. Recipes in this book use the power levels below as stated for a Panasonic NN-6405 900-watt microwave oven. The power levels and uses are a guide only – check the instruction booklet of your own microwave oven and adjust accordingly.

Power levels	Power	Guide to use
HIGH	100%	Boil water, cook fresh fruit, vegetables, rice and pasta. Reheat soups, stews, casseroles.
MEDIUM-HIGH	70%	Cook poultry, meat, cakes, desserts. Heat milk.
MEDIUM	55%	Cook pot roasts, casseroles and meatloaves. Melt chocolate. Cook eggs and cheese. Cook fish.
MEDIUM-LOW	30%	Simmer soups, stews and casseroles (less tender cuts). Soften butter and cream cheese.
DEFROST	30%	Thaw foods.
LOW	10%	Keep cooked foods warm, simmer slowly.

how to measure

When using graduated metric measuring cups, shake dry ingredients loosely into the appropriate cup. Do not tap the cup on a bench or tightly pack the ingredients unless directed to do so. Level top of measuring cups and measuring spoons with a knife. When measuring liquids, place a clear glass or plastic jug with metric markings on a flat surface to check accuracy at eye level.

Looking after your interest...

Keep your Home Library cookbooks clean, tidy and within easy reach
with slipcovers designed to hold up to 12 books. *Plus* you can follow our recipes perfectly
with a set of accurate measuring cups and spoons, as used by the Women's Weekly Test Kitchen

TO ORDER

Mail or fax Photocopy or complete the coupon below and post or fax to AWW Home Library Reader Offer, ACP Direct, PO Box 7036, Sydney NSW 1028 or fax to (02) 9267 4363.

Credit cards Have your details ready, Sydney: (02) 9260 0000; elsewhere in Australia: 1800 252 515 (free call, Mon-Fri, 8.30am-5.30pm).

PRICE

Book Holder $11.95 (Australia); elsewhere $A21.95.

Metric Measuring Set $5.95 (Australia); $A8.00 (New Zealand); $A9.95 elsewhere. Prices include postage and handling. This offer is available in all countries.

PAYMENT

Australian residents We accept the credit cards listed, money orders and cheques.

Overseas residents We accept the credit cards listed, drafts in $A drawn on an Australian bank, and also British, New Zealand and U.S. cheques in the currency of the country of issue. Credit card charges are at the exchange rate current at the time of payment.

❑ **BOOK HOLDER** ❑ **METRIC MEASURING SET**

Please indicate number(s) required.

Mr/Mrs/Ms ______________________________

Address ______________________________

____

Postcode ______________ Country ______________

Ph: Bus. Hours:( ) ______________________________

I enclose my cheque/money order for $ ______________ payable to ACP Direct

OR: please charge my:

❑ Bankcard ❑ Visa ❑ MasterCard ❑ Diners Club ❑ Amex

Expiry Date ____/____

Cardholder's signature ______________________________

Please allow up to 30 days for delivery within Australia. Allow up to 6 weeks for overseas deliveries. Both offers expire 31/12/99.
HLEMIC99